PRAISE FO

Spiritual formation and the d~~~~~~ ~~ ~~~
Christians they have little to do with each other. That's why *Shape Shifters* is such an important book. What Derek Vreeland has done here is to connect the dots, showing us how vitally and inextricably bound together they are. The Trinitarian vision of spiritual transformation he sets forth is biblical, balanced, and beautiful. It will resonate with Christians from various traditions and will surely benefit the whole Church. Read it and be informed, inspired, and transformed.

> —Dr. Stephen Seamands
> Professor of Christian Doctrine, Asbury Theological Seminary
> Wilmore, Kentucky

Derek Vreeland has done a great job in *Shape Shifters* by giving the church a sound biblical and theological view of spiritual transformation in the lives of Jesus followers. This book is not just lofty thinking. Derek joins good doctrine to practical living which makes this book a valuable resource to individual believers and local congregations. I was highly encouraged in my own reading to submit myself to the work of the Holy Spirit's work to conform me to the image of Christ for the joy of God the Father. I cannot wait to use this book in my local church! Read this book with others in your church—it will bring great benefit and blessing.

> —Rev. Rodney A. Bradford
> Pastor, Arabi Baptist Church
> Arabi, Georgia

With his book *Shape Shifters*, Derek Vreeland makes an excellent contribution to the important subject of spiritual transformation—a subject which has been largely ignored within in the Charismatic and Pentecostal community. Instead of parodying the self-help methods that characterize the pseudo-spiritual culture of contemporary America, *Shape Shifters* gives us a well-written exploration of spiritual transformation founded in solid, historic, Trinitarian theology. We live in a time when there is a tendency to dismiss theology as unimportant and irrelevant. The truth is everyone does theology. We either do it well or we do it poorly. Derek Vreeland is a pastor who does theology well and does it with relevance. If you have a hunger for genuine spiritual transformation that the shallow self-help gimmicks fail to satisfy, I enthusiastically recommend Derek Vreeland's substantive and compelling book.

> —Pastor Brian Zahnd
> Senior Pastor, Word of Life Church
> St. Joseph, Missouri

SHAPE SHIFTERS

HOW GOD CHANGES THE HUMAN HEART

A Trinitarian Vision of
Spiritual Transformation

DEREK VREELAND

WORD & SPIRIT PRESS
TULSA, OKLAHOMA

Shape Shifters: How God Changes the Human Heart: A Trinitarian Vision of Spiritual Transformation

Copyright © 2008 by Derek Vreeland
http://www.derekvreeland.com

Printed in the United States of America if bought from there. Printed in the United Kingdom if bought from there.

Scripture quotations marked (NIV) are taken from the HOLY BIBLE, NEW INTERNATIONAL VERSION®. NIV®. Copyright © 1973, 1978, 1984 by International Bible Society. Used by permission of Zondervan. All rights reserved.

Scripture quotations marked (NKJV) are taken from the New King James Version®. NKJV™. Copyright © 1982 by Thomas Nelson, Inc. Used by permission. All rights reserved.

Published in Tulsa, Oklahoma, by Word & Spirit Press
WordSP@gmail.com • http://WandSP.com

Book design and composition by Bob Bubnis / Booksetters, Bowling Green, Kentucky

ISBN 10: 0-9785352-9-4 [paperback]
ISBN 13: 978-0-9785352-9-2

∞ The paper used in this publication meets the minimum requirements of the American National Standard for Information Sciences—Permanence of Paper for Printed Library Materials, ANSI Z39.48-1992.

CONTENTS

DEDICATION

To Jenni
My love, my friend, my partner

And to Wesley and Taylor
May the Holy Spirit continue to transform you both
into the image of Jesus for the joy of God the Father
in the context of Christian community
as you learn to walk along spiritual pathways

ACKNOWLEDGEMENTS

This book would not have been possible without the input, support, and assistance of so many people. I want to express my deepest thanks to the following friends:

Jenni—Nothing in my life would be possible without your love and support.

Steve Seamands—Your passion for the doctrine of the Trinity has shaped me in profound ways.

Brian Zahnd—Many of the ideas and imagery in this book are the fruit from the seeds you have planted in me.

Darrell Chatraw—Your prayers and encouragement over the years have helped steady the course on my journey of spiritual transformation.

Rebekah Daniel—Your careful editing and thoughtful suggestions made my writing better than it is.

Mark Roberts—Thank you not only for publishing the book, but for your helpful suggestions in shaping the book into what it has become.

Mom, Dad, Jeff, and Jenny—Thank you for your encouragement and support in this writing project.

The Cornerstone Church Family—Many of the concepts in this book were hashed out in home group discussions, breakfast meetings, conversations over lunch, and during countless sermons. Thank you for loving me through my deficiencies, encouraging me in my strengths, and giving me the wonderful freedom to pursue God's purpose for my life. May we continue to grow together in the love and grace of the Father, Son, and Holy Spirit.

INTRODUCTION

Now the nature of man is to beg and to steal
I'd do it myself it's not so unreal
The call of the wild's forever at my door
Want me to fly like an eagle while being chained to the floor,
But you changed my life

— BOB DYLAN —

Various cultures throughout the centuries have told stories of shape shifters as a part of their folklore. Shape shifters have been depicted as people, animals, or some kind of mythic creature. They have appeared in Homer's *The Odyssey*, throughout Greek mythology, Celtic mythology, British fairy tales, and various forms of Asian folklore. In popular American culture, modern shape shifters appear in various werewolf tales, in the beloved children's story *The Beauty and The Beast*, in the ever-popular *Shrek* series, and in various science fiction series like *Star Trek: Deep Space Nine*. Collectively, we seem to have an interest in human beings (and mythological creatures) who can change form, who can shift from one shape to another.

My all-time favorite book as a child was *Leaf Magic* by New Zealand author Margaret Mahy. My mom read *Leaf Magic* to me over and over when I was a child. It always captured my attention at bedtime. In the story, a young boy, Michael, wants a dog. Instead of a furry friend, he somehow finds himself being followed around by a big orange leaf. This leaf follows him everywhere he goes. He feels pestered by the leaf and frustrated without a dog. The story climaxes with a surprise encounter with an eccentric old man who is able to transform the big orange leaf into a dog

13

through a mystical trunk. I can still remember pictures in *Leaf Magic* of Michael dancing with his shape-shifting leaf-dog.

Fairy tales from our childhood have a powerful way of shaping the way we look at life as adults. Too often we make the mistake of disregarding childhood fairy tales in favor of the so-called real world. G.K. Chesterton, in his monumental work, *Orthodoxy*, affirms the surpassing value of fairyland. He writes,

> *My first and last philosophy, that which I believe in with unbroken certainty, I learnt in the nursery. I generally learnt it from a nurse; that is, from the solemn and star-appointed priestess at once of democracy and tradition. The things I believed most then, the things I believe most now, are the things called fairy tales. They seem to me to be the entirely reasonable things.*[1]

Fairy tales and folklore have a way of shaping the way we look at reality. As an adult, they create in me the belief that we can become shape shifters. In the face of the growing cynicism which says, "People never change," I believe we *can* change and become different people. As followers of Jesus, we can readily expect to experience shape-shifting of a different variety, the spiritual shaping on the inside from a cold heart of stone to a heart of flesh brimming with life and vitality.

I have written this book out of my own journey. It has been a spiritual and theological journey to become a shape shifter, to understanding how the Triune God shapes my inner character to reflect the character of Christ. I write as a fellow pilgrim, a fellow sojourner climbing this mountain of Christian experience. I have not attained full-blown shape shifter status, but I continue to press on. I want to shift into the shape of Jesus and help others do the same, because one of the purposes of God's salvation is transformation—spiritual transformation now and physical transformation when Jesus returns.

I have devoted my life to seeing God's gospel transform hearts, families, and communities around the world. My work is for the benefit of the local church, the visible and mystical body of Christ carrying out the mission of Jesus. My personal shape-shifting journey has grown out of tearful sorrow at the growing number of moral failures, particularly in Christian leadership in the United States. Immorality, pride, ambition, greed, envy, and sins of a sordid variety have begun to rip the soul out of the heart of the Church in the United States. Whenever I hear stories of Christian leaders who have fallen under the weight of their own sin, it strikes a mournful chord within me. It causes me to reflect on my own sinfulness, and I realize my own ability to stumble and fall. It drives me to become a shape shifter all the more, until I become a living, breathing, expression of Jesus.

I have not written to judge those who have fallen. *Before their own Master they will stand or fall.* I have written out of my personal spiritual exploration in order to help other people discover God's work in restoring the human soul and reshaping the human heart to resemble the heart of him who was crucified, buried, and who is now risen and alive. As I have explored this shape-shifting journey of becoming like Jesus, I have found footing in the doctrine of the Trinity. Nearly all Christians profess a belief in the Trinity, but they live as if God is singular. We maintain Trinitarian language in our statements of faith, our creeds, and even, at times, in our worship music and liturgy. Yet many of us have not been able to incorporate the doctrine of the Trinity into our everyday lives.

I have pursued Jesus in an active relationship for nearly two decades. Most of the Christians I have encountered during this time live completely oblivious to the wealth of spiritual experience waiting in an exploration of God as one holy community of Father, Son, and Holy Spirit. My rediscovery of God as the Trinity has been the most important and the most invigorating chapter in the story of my Christian pilgrimage. It has given me a new way to look at worship, ministry, and especially spiritual transformation. This book is the explosive combination of my own great need for spiritual transformation and my rediscovery of the Trinity. I invite you to join me on this spiritual exploration as we seek to become shape shifters, changing into the image of Jesus, by the Holy Spirit, for the joy of God the Father in the context of Christian community.

Chapter One

A SPIRITUALITY OF CHANGE

Therefore, having become His disciples, let us learn to live according to the principles of Christianity. For whosoever is called by any other name besides this, is not of God. Lay aside, therefore, the evil, the old, the sour leaven, and be ye changed into the new leaven, which is Jesus Christ.

— IGNATIUS OF ANTIOCH —

Change is hard. If you do not think so, then just try to change your diet. My wife has been on a low carb kick for a couple of years. When she started losing weight, I thought I would give it a try. Like most American men, I wanted to lose a little weight around the midsection. I thought, "How hard can this low carb diet be? I can give up bread, rice, and potatoes as long as I can eat meat." Then I started what one low carb diet calls "induction," or what I like to call "a two-week trip to the dark underworld." This simple change in diet quickly became a painfully complex quandary. Gone were the quick bowls of cereal. Gone were the snacks of potato chips. Gone were the quick stops at local fast food restaurants. All of a sudden, instead of eating whatever I wanted, whenever I wanted, I was under a self-imposed regulation. I had to plan out my meals ahead of time. I had to think through dinner invitations from friends. *Were they going to serve anything I could eat?* Then came the cravings. I soon began dreaming of Krispy Kreme donuts and chicken fried rice. During this time, I would have traded a major bodily organ for a single slice of enriched flour, white bread. Change is not easy. It is impeccably difficult.

Jesus calls us into a life in his kingdom where change is not optional. He requires a lifestyle of change. Jesus told his followers, "I tell you the truth, unless you change and become like little children, you will never enter the kingdom of heaven" (Matthew 18:3). I can imagine Peter and John cutting their eyes at each other with competitive looks, thinking to themselves that acting like a child will make this whole entrance into the kingdom a whole lot easier. However, Jesus did not tell them that acting like a child was the way into the kingdom. He said they must change and become child-like. Change preceded the child-likeness.

We can much more easily envision the end result of our transformation than to consider the process of change leading us toward it. The destination of our transformation is exactly what Jesus told us—the purity and innocence of child-likeness. Consider the ease of childhood. No baggage. No responsibilities. No worries. A return to a place of innocence is certainly appealing, but child-likeness is the destination of our journey, not the journey itself. The journey of change is a winding, meandering road filled with potholes, unexpected twists and turns, and frustrating setbacks. It takes Jesus one sentence to describe the pathway into the kingdom of God, but it takes us a lifetime to walk its path.

The change Jesus spoke of is central to his message and his movement. The word he used most often used to describe this change is the word "repent." Jesus began his life as a preacher with a three-phrase sermon, "The time is fulfilled, and the kingdom of God is at hand; repent and believe in the gospel" (Mark 1:15). The Greek word "repent" is *metanoeite*, which means "change your mind." In view of God's kingdom, Jesus was saying, "Reframe your thinking about yourself and life in relation to God and allow this reorientation to fuel your faith." To state it more bluntly, Jesus was saying, "Change!"

Above all other themes, change became the message of the movement. The followers of Jesus were sent out by their Master with specific instructions. Jesus told them not to take anything when they went out except a staff and a good pair of walking sandals. As their sandal-clad feet carried them from town to town, they proclaimed the message of the Master. They told people to repent, to change, to reframe their thinking in terms of God's kingdom.[1]

Peter, the obnoxious, loud-mouth fisherman turned loud-mouth Christ-follower, was filled with the Holy Spirit along with the other disciples after the ascension of Jesus. In the chaotic moments that followed, he stood in front of a large crowd and boldly told people that the Jesus who had been killed was both the Son of God and the King. His startling revelation struck deep in the hearts of the crowd. They asked what they must do, and Peter began his response with one word—*repent*.[2] Peter preached the same message his Master preached. If a person wanted to join the Jesus revolution and enter into God's kingdom, change was required.

Jesus reminds his followers that change is necessary when he appeared to John in the apocalyptic vision recorded in the Book of Revelation. Jesus appeared to John in a mystical vision and told him to write a letter to the First Apostolic Church of Ephesus. In the letter, Jesus told John to tell the church in Ephesus that he (Jesus) knew what they had been doing, that they had been working hard and hanging in there.[3] Then came the bad news: Jesus had one thing against them. They had abandoned their first love. In the letter, Jesus asks them to remember the heights of their former passion for him and then reminds them of the one-word slogan of his movement—*repent*. He appealed to them to change, to reorient their loveless lives of hard work around the loveliness of the Son of God.

CHANGING BY DYING

We enter the kingdom of God through the doorway of change, and when we get sidetracked, change is the checkpoint. We do not express the Christian faith without the work of change. We cannot offer an acceptable act of worship without the sacrifice of change. Jesus used a vivid metaphor to describe the change required in his kingdom. Of all the imagery he could have used, he chose a violent picture in calling his followers to change. He said *take up your cross*.

Crucifixion had become a common means of execution in the Roman-occupied province of Galilee. Crucifixion was brutal and hideous, a very public statement of Roman authority. As Jews would walk along the road and see the repulsive sight of a bloody, twisted human figure, gasping for breath, the message was clear: "Do not mess with Rome." The cross was not the religious emblem that we have come to know in modern times. The cross was emblematic of only one thing—death.

Jesus did not morbidly fixate on death, because death was not a conclusion, but a beginning. When Jesus said, "If anyone would come after me, he must deny himself and take up his cross daily and follow me," (Luke 9:23), he wanted death to be daily, but not the end result of our faith. Death through the metaphorical cross marked the end of the old life and the beginning of the changed life. Dietrich Bonhoeffer rightly noted,

> *The cross is not the terrible end to an otherwise godfearing [sic] and happy life, but it meets us at the beginning of our communion with Christ. When Christ calls a man, he bids him come and die.*[4]

Death through the self-denying cross is the Jesus way of change. We change by dying.

A Spirituality of Change

We change both through momentary events and through a long process. Change is both individual and communal, ancient and future. As we pass through corridors of change, we move into a certain kind of spirituality, a life lived in the Spirit. People often stumble when trying to describe spirituality. Most definitions of spirituality are clumsy and ambiguous. It is one of those culturally fluid and religiously laden words. I can describe it better than I can define it. "Spirituality" includes transcendence, going beyond oneself, and living out one's humanity to its fullest. [5]

In terms of *Christian* spirituality, the word describes a human life lived in the Holy Spirit. Gordon Fee notes that any biblical concept of spirituality is undoubtedly grounded in the Holy Spirit. He writes, "One is spiritual to the degree that one lives in and walks by the Spirit; in Scripture the word [spirituality] has no other meaning, and no other measurement."[6] Spirituality is the way in which we experience life in the Holy Spirit, and within the Christian life we experience a spirituality of change. We undergo a shape-shifting process of change through death into a new life, a fully human life.

Paul does not use the word "repent" in his letters that make up nearly two-thirds of the New Testament.[7] He uses a different word in various forms to communicate the same process of change. He uses the Greek word *morpho,* from which we get the English word "morph," or "metamorphosis" meaning "to transform." In Greek literature, the various forms of this word meant "to take on the form, to be formed, or to be shaped." It was used to describe the formation of a human embryo in the womb. *Morpho* would vividly describe the miraculous process of an embryo transforming from a mass of cells bursting forth with unique DNA into the physical shape of a human baby.

Human development is an unimaginable miracle. I remember sitting in the doctor's office and watching the ultrasound pictures of my first son while he was still in my wife's womb. I remember anxiously staring at that black and white screen unable to determine what was baby and what was grainy, black splotches. When the doctor began to point out arms and legs and the baby's head, I was amazed. There was a little person in there! What started out as a small fertilized egg was now a baby ready to be born. I am still astounded that God has created women with the ability to carry a baby inside their wombs. By a miraculously passive process, babies grow through the states of gestation, shifting from one shape to another. My sons were not in their mother's womb with surgical instruments putting themselves together. Rather, cells multiplied time and time again following their own genetic code. All my sons had to do was hang on for the ride.

We can clearly see the meaning of the Greek word *morph* when we talk about the metamorphosis of a caterpillar into a butterfly. Think about the life of a geometrid caterpillar, also known as the inchworm. Our friend the caterpillar lives a sad linear existence. In order to get from point A to point B, a caterpillar has to walk a straight line, and this is no easy task. He has to bend his body nearly in half in order to move in a certain direction. Then one day he spins himself into a cocoon and waits. When the time is right, he breaks out of the cocoon as a new creature. The process of metamorphosis has made him into a butterfly, freeing him from the confines of a linear existence.[8] He is now free to move in a variety of directions at speeds he never dreamed possible. He has gone from riding a tricycle to flying on a jet airplane. He has morphed. His shape has shifted. He has been changed.

SPIRITUAL TRANSFORMATION

Paul uses this Greek word *morpho* in various forms in four different places in Scripture to describe shape-shifting change.

For those God foreknew he also predestined to be conformed to the likeness of his Son, that he might be the firstborn among many brothers. (Romans 8:29)

21

Do not conform any longer to the pattern of this world, but be transformed by the renewing of your mind. Then you will be able to test and approve what God's will is—his good, pleasing and perfect will. (Romans 12:2)

And we, who with unveiled faces all reflect the Lord's glory, are being transformed into his likeness with ever-increasing glory, which comes from the Lord, who is the Spirit. (2 Corinthians 3:18)

My dear children, for whom I am again in the pains of childbirth until Christ is formed in you. (Galatians 4:19)

Twice he uses the word "transformed," once he uses the word "conformed" and once he uses the word "formed." All of these uses of the word *morpho* refer to what we now call spiritual formation or spiritual transformation.

I prefer to use the term *transformation* over *formation*, because even before God saves us and we become Christians, our hearts have been formed into one shape or another.[9] Our family relationships, educational environments, friends, bullies, various forms of media, and exposure to spiritual ideas have all played their parts in forming our hearts into a certain shape. This process of change described by Paul consists in transforming us from the shape we are in currently into a new form constructed as we live in a vital relationship with God.

The *spiritual* part of spiritual transformation has also given people trouble as they try to understand how God changes them. There are three common ways people interpret spiritual transformation. People commonly describe spiritual transformation as (1) the practice of the classic spiritual disciplines or other particular religious practices, (2) the shaping of the inner life, or (3) shaping by the Holy Spirit.[10] The practice of spiritual disciplines like prayer, silence, fasting, and study are essential components to spiritual transformation, but they are not the *thing* itself. These practices are a part to the entire puzzle, but spiritual transformation is something bigger than devotional practices.

A number of different religions and ideologies offer practices to shape one's heart. Oprah includes a "remembering your spirit" segment on *The Oprah Winfrey Show* and discusses transforming your life in the "Self and Spirit" section of her webpage.[11] Very often these are filled with helpful habits that lead people to a transformed life, but not a *Christian* transformed life. These first two descriptions do not get at the heart of spiritual transformation in the Christian spiritual tradition. For followers of Christ, spiritual transformation is the shaping of our hearts by the Holy Spirit.

When Paul discusses spiritual transformation, he uses the word *morpho* in a passive sense, implying that we are not the ones who change ourselves. When he wrote to the gathering of Christ followers in Galatia, he did not write, "My dear children, for whom I am again in the pains of childbirth until *you get off your lazy duffs and start forming yourself into the image of Christ!*" Have you ever heart anyone describe spiritual transformation or Christian discipleship in that way? Haven't you heard this process of change, repentance, or transformation described in terms of what you have to do?

I cannot place a face with the voice, but I can still hear a guilt-laden voice in the back of my head saying, "*You need to spend more time reading your Bible. You need to pray more, work harder, and go to church more often. You want to watch a football game on TV...what?!? It is a good thing Jesus was not thinking about football when he was dying on the cross for your sins!*"

Is this what the voice of God sounds like?

Is everything in my journey of transformation up to me and my ability to change myself by working harder, and engaging in my church activities? When did we stumble upon the idea that transformation was all up to us? Why do Christian leaders and teachers feel the need to place the entire burden of transformation on people and their ability?

As one of the early leaders of the Christian movement, Paul did not put pressure on people to change themselves. He expected followers of Christ to fulfill their responsibility to walk down certain spiritual pathways in order to work out their own salvation. He expected them to strip off the old life in order to walk in the new life on the Jesus way. Nevertheless he felt the pain and pressure as a leader to see the people in his care become transformed. He compared this pressure to the pain a woman goes through in natural childbirth. The agony Paul felt as a leader was real, but it was not a pressure derived from thinking he had to transform them. He did not say he was in the pains of childbirth until *he did the work of forming Christ in them*. Rather he told them that he was in pain until "Christ is formed in you" (Galatians 4:19). Paul's responsibility included the forming and transforming, but it was not accomplished by his direct action. The power transform the human heart resides in another.

When people talk about spiritual transformation solely in terms of the shaping of our inner life, they are not necessarily talking about Christian spiritual transformation. A lot of external influences can be about the work of shaping our inner lives. We are formed in part by cultural influences. This kind of forming can be good and bad. Obviously, there are negative influences in our culture shaping us into a form that does not please God, but certain influences which do not bear a Christian label can be positive. Developing a person's self-esteem is positive, although it is not necessarily Christian in nature. Spiritual transformation in the Christian tradition is the work of the Holy Spirit, and not the direct effort of any human participant.

The Holy Spirit works like the hands of God shaping our hearts like a potter who shapes a cold lump clay into a beautiful piece of pottery. Jesus the Son of God is the model, the perfect example of a man fully human and fully alive, living in perfect obedience. The Spirit is the master craftsman, transforming us from the deformed image left by sin into the blemishless image of Jesus. I have observed a growing interest in spiritual transformation as related to discipleship and spiritual growth in recent years. The beauty of this blossoming discussion is that it is not univocal, but ecumenical in nature. People have joined the conversation from various denominations and Christian traditions, including:

- *Dallas Willard, a Southern Baptist, has been a catalyst in this renewed interest in spiritual transformation. His Renovation of the Heart (2002) is a helpful overview of spiritual transformation.*

- *Richard Foster, a Quaker, published the highly influential Celebration of Discipline (1978). His current ministry, Renovare, is spreading the passion for spiritual transformation across denominational lines.*

- *Eugene Peterson, has influenced many church leaders outside of his Presbyterian tradition through many of his books, including Long Obedience in the Same Direction (1980), Working the Angles: The Shape of Pastoral Integrity (1987), and Eat This Book (2006).*

- *Robert Mulholland Jr., who teaches New Testament studies at the Wesleyan-oriented Asbury Theological Seminary, has written on the subject of spiritual formation in Invitation to a Journey (1993) and The Deeper Journey (2006).*

The one group that is surprisingly quiet in this conversation is the Pentecostal/charismatic tradition, which has been an integral part to my growth in Christ. No other group has more to offer and more to gain from a focus on spiritual transformation. The moral failures of certain predominate, media-driven Pentecostal/charismatic leaders in the late 1980s brought to light Pentecostalism's "dark side,"[12] including a rampant departure from the movement's holiness roots. Charismatic Christians have a lot to gain from a renewed focus on spiritual transformation. This group is also in the best position to add a substantial contribution to the ecumenical dialogue on the subject of spiritual transformation because much of the Pentecostal/charismatic movement is oriented around the Holy Spirit.[13]

Spiritual transformation is an ecumenical dialogue because it is the spirituality of discipleship shared by all those whom God has saved, called, and empowered with his Holy Spirit. Regardless of our individual, nonessential doctrinal positions and our various church traditions, we who bear the name of Christ desire to be transformed into his image. We may disagree on how the Holy Spirit is at work, but we share a confession concerning the Holy Spirit who is "the Lord, the giver of life who proceeds from the Father and the Son."[14] We share a common desire to experience the Spirit's shape-shifting work, a work to make us more human, more fully alive, more like Jesus.

STUDY GUIDE

1. What has been one of the hardest things to change in your life?

2. How do you want the Holy Spirit to transform you? Do you think Peter was surprised by the change in his own heart?

3. What desire, craving, or bad habit do you need to die to?

4. What have been major influences in molding your heart to its shape before God saved you?

5. Do you feel you are living a linear existence of a caterpillar where the Christian life seems predictable and boring, or are you living the limitless existence of a butterfly where the Christian life is full of freedom and adventure? Why?

6. Why is it so hard to be passive and allow the Holy Spirit to change you? Why is it that we typically want to work to change ourselves?

7. What have been your experiences with denominations other than your own, and how might they enhance your understanding of spiritual transformation?

Chapter Two

SPIRITUAL DIMENSIONS

*Ye know that the great end of religion is, to renew our
hearts in the image of God, to repair that total loss of
righteousness and true holiness which we sustained by the
sin of our first parent. Ye know that all religion which does
not answer this end, all that stops short of this, the renewal
of our soul in the image of God, after the likeness of Him
that created it, is no other than a poor farce, and a mere
mockery of God, to the destruction of our own soul.*

— JOHN WESLEY —

The shape-shifting work of the Holy Spirit is at the core of the various
spiritual dimensions of the Christian life. Spiritual transformation is
the heartbeat of Christian spirituality. In Western culture, it has become
common for people to disassociate the practice of religion from spirituality. You can often hear people say, "I am not really religious, but I am
spiritual." Often people equate *religion* with external rules, rituals, and
regulations, while being *spiritual* is something quite different, something
internal and experiential. As human beings, we have the ability not only to
love, cry, laugh, feel, think, reflect, and imagine, but to experience a spiritual component of ourselves that is able to come in contact with something
outside the material and rational world. For those who put their faith and
confidence in Jesus, that something is a Someone—the triune God. Christian spirituality as framed by Scripture is therefore an active relationship
with this God, specifically in, with, and by the Holy Spirit.

There are numerous areas of Christian spirituality where the Holy
Spirit is at work. The Spirit illuminates the Scripture as we spend time

reading God's word. The Spirit sets us free from the past and empowers us to live as new creatures with pure motivations and right hearts. The Holy Spirit ignites our hearts with unending passion for God. The Holy Spirit gives gifts for service, so we can serve the Christian community and contribute in the world where God precedes us in the work of re-demption. The Spirit unites our hearts with other followers of Christ, forming us into a loving community. He empowers us to speak on God's behalf by telling God's redemptive story through our own stories. These encounters and interactions with the Holy Spirit are spiritual dimen-sions, true reflections of Christian spirituality, but they are each con-nected to the Holy Spirit's primary work of shaping and transforming our hearts.

Each spiritual dimension draws its source from this central, shape-shifting work of the Spirit. There are at least six distinct spiritual dimen-sions that draw life from spiritual transformation. It is tempting to make any one of these six dimensions the central component to Christian spiri-tuality, but to do so will cause us to become unbalanced in our relationship with God. These six interrelated dimensions are *doctrine, ethics, devotion, service, mission,* and *community.* While each one is a necessary compo-nent to the experiential Christian life, no single one of them can be the central focus of our life with God. We can only stay centered and stable with transformation at the heart of our Christian life.

Over the years, I have noticed that my spiritual journey begins to take a detour anytime I allow one of the six to become the focus of my spiritual pursuits. Normally my detour has begun when I have come under the influ-ence of a certain teachers, writers, or Christian thinkers who place some-thing other than spiritual transformation in the forefront of their particular brand of Christian spirituality. During my days in college, I was under the primary influence of devotional writers and thinkers who focused me on a spirituality of devotion. I was focused, not on becoming more like Jesus, but on the practices of private and public worship. I was determined not just to worship, but to worship God *correctly* as narrowly defined by out-wardly demonstrative expressions. As I look back, I see that I was not so much enraptured in a life-changing relationship with the triune God as I was enraptured with the rush of emotionally-driven forms of private prayer and corporate worship. Devotion had taken the center seat of my spiritual-ity. Transformation was secondary and, honestly, non-existent during those years. I was more interested in spiritual encounters with the Holy Spirit than spiritual transformation.

In my seminary years after college, I shifted from devotion to doctrine. My introduction to the world of academic theology quickly brought doctrine to the center stage in my spirituality. I am overwhelmingly appreciative for the two seminary experiences I have had. They both guided my thinking, giving me an insightful perspective on the Scripture, ministry, relationships, and, of course, God. Without my seminary journeys, my window into the divine life would have been unfortunately narrow. Nevertheless, life in academic study in my first seminary experience pushed devotion to the side in order to make doctrine central. During this time, I concluded that to be a spiritual person and to walk rightly in God's Spirit required a passionate pursuit of doctrine—biblical, historical, and orthodox doctrine. Just as with devotion, the goal was not so much to become like Jesus; it was simply to reach the point where my thinking had become theologically mature. The work of study and pursuing right doctrine is essential, but it reduces the work of the Spirit. The Holy Spirit has come not only to guide us into all truth, but he has come to transform our whole lives, so that we reflect the image of Jesus in our thinking and in our motivations and in our attitudes. At various times in my spiritual journey, I have found myself off center.

Each spiritual dimension has a corresponding question that helps us understand the nature of the dimension itself and the work of the Spirit within it. Questions are not attempts to subvert tradition. Questions help us dig through the surface into the depths and richness of spiritual experience. When asked out of humility and respect for the Scriptures and the historic Christian faith, questions lead us to a more intimate relationship with God and deeper levels of transformation. The question for each dimension becomes our guide in pursuing the Spirit's work. The questions are:

- *Doctrine: "What do we believe?"*

- *Ethics: "How do we live?"*

- *Devotion: "How do we worship?"*

- *Service: "What do we do for others?"*

- *Mission: "How do we communicate the gospel message?"*

- *Community: "Who are we doing life with?"*

- *Transformation: "Who are we becoming?"*

DOCTRINE: "WHAT DO WE BELIEVE?"

The English word "doctrine" comes from the Latin word *doctrina* meaning "teaching, instruction, knowledge, or learning." Doctrines are those key tenets of the faith we have been taught in the church. Doctrine asks the question, "What do we believe?" The Holy Spirit works to create this truth. It was the Spirit who inspired the Scripture upon which our doctrine is built. The Holy Spirit also leads and guides us into all truth.[1] He illuminates the Scripture as we lay it open, and he helps us understand both what the text meant and what it means. The pursuit of right doctrine is a crucial part of our Christian life and is a critical mission of the Holy Spirit. It is crucial, but not central. Some Christians centralize doctrine and become Bible-thumping know-it-alls who do more damage than good for the kingdom of God.

Pursuing a right understanding of Christian doctrine shapes how we live the Christian life. We live out of what we believe. Our internal statement of faith becomes a filter by which we discern right from wrong and truth from error. It gives us boundaries in which to explore both the Creator and his creation. It is not always practical. Some elements of Christian doctrine are not instantly applicable to your life. More than anything, the pursuit of doctrine keeps you focused on God's agenda and purposes for life. It may not always be practical, but Christian doctrine is rigorously experiential. We do not merely think about what we believe; we encounter it. As doctrine works to focus us on God's agenda, we are brought in contact with the living God, the maker of heaven and earth. God is not just a subject to be studied, but a person to interact with and a living entity to experience. *Still, right doctrine, though important, is not central.*

ETHICS: "HOW DO WE LIVE?"

When Jesus called his original disciples, his call was not "come *believe* me," but "come *follow* me." Christian spirituality is not merely an intellectual exercise; it must be lived out in time and space in a dynamic relationship with God. Jesus came to blaze a trail, a way of living in right relationship with people, creation, and the Creator. We most certainly need Jesus to rescue us from our sins and the wasteland of our own fallenness. We cannot merely stroll along the Jesus way and expect to arrive in the kingdom of God. We need God's merciful hands of forgiveness to rescue us through the death, burial, and resurrection of Jesus. We are utterly dependent upon God for salvation, but being rescued from sin is not the conclusion of God's salvation; it is the beginning. God saves us in order to transform us and place us on the Jesus way. Jesus said, "I am the way and the truth and the life" (John 14:6). Walking along the Jesus way is living the Jesus life by becoming transformed into his image.

Walking the Jesus way is a daunting task. Living a life patterned by his involves more than simple imitation. In order to live life like Jesus requires the very life of God. He gave us access to the Jesus way by giving himself in the person of Christ in order to rescue us from sin and judgment. After giving himself through Christ, God gave himself in his life-giving Spirit, so we could walk the Jesus way. The Holy Spirit becomes our guide, our moral compass through the world littered with pitfalls and obstacles. By the Spirit, we are able to choose truth from error and righteousness from sin. As we live according to the Spirit, and set our minds on the Spirit, we will live according to what the Spirit desires (Romans 8:5). The way forward out of any moral dilemma is the careful guidance of the Holy Spirit. In this, Christian spirituality becomes undoubtedly practical. The degree to which we do right and speak right is in direct relation to the degree we are surrendered, yielded, empowered, controlled, filled, and led by the Holy Spirit. *Still, ethics, though important, are not central.*

DEVOTION: "HOW DO WE WORSHIP?

God created us for worship. We need to avoid the mistake of confusing worship with religion in reference to devotion. Religion with its rituals, traditions, social structures, and written codes contains worshipful elements. However worship does not require a religious context. We do not need rituals and religious creeds to worship. *What has captured your heart? What are you really passionate about? Where do you invest your money? What do you insatiably talk about? What really excites you?* As you begin to answer these questions, you will begin to see what (or who) you worship. Devotion is whenever you give your heart away to another. Often when people speak of a married couple who are deeply in love, they will describe how devoted they are to each other. Devotion is a passionate giving away of your heart in loyal dedication to another.

Christian worship as practiced by the Church, and rooted in Scripture, requires honest and authentic devotion. Passionless praise is no praise at all. Worship with the lips without the corresponding devotion of the heart is empty hypocrisy. It is play acting. Jesus described heartless, passionless worship as merely holding onto traditions, but letting go of the commandments of God (Mark 7:8). Paul described it as "having a form of godliness but denying its power" (2 Timothy 3:5). Devotion in the Christian community that is contrived or achieved by manipulation or guilt seldom lasts a lifetime. Real spiritual devotion is the overflow of the Spirit-filled life. The faithful followers of Jesus in Ephesus were counseled to be continually filled with the Holy Spirit which would result in psalms, hymns, spiritual songs, and making heart music (devotion) to the Lord.[2] The Holy Spirit fuels our devotion so we can be fervent in Spirit. *Still, devotion, though important, is not central.*

Service: "What do we do for others?"

Christian spirituality in its purest form can be defined in terms of love—not the sappy, sentimental kind of love shared on greeting cards, but love communicated by stripping down to your skivvies, wrapping yourself in a towel, and washing nasty, stinky feet. I never understood how incredibly loathsome washing feet in Jesus' day must have been until my first trip to India. I was walking down a paved road in a small Indian town in Andhra Pradesh, when I looked over my shoulder and noticed a herd of Asian buffalo walking up the road behind me. I stopped on the side of the road and watched the young shepherds lead them on up the road. In the chaotic beauty of Indian road traffic everything (and everybody) uses the same roads—people on foot, bicycles, motorcycles, rickshaws, jeeps, buses, and yes, animals. The Asian buffalo I saw that day bustled their way up the road, and they did not stop for anything. There were no restroom stops for the herd. They did their business right on the road.

I wonder if the roads where similarly shared by people and animals in Jesus' day? If they were, then sandal-wearing Jews at that time would have picked up all kinds of grime as they walked the dusty roads surrounding Jerusalem. Jesus' washing his disciple's feet was no sponge bath. He washed unspeakable filth from their feet and dried them with the very towel with which he covered himself. He then tells his followers to go about the business of washing each other's feet. According to Jesus, love is going the extra mile, turning the other cheek, washing feet, caring, and looking to serve others. The Holy Spirit empowers such service. The Spirit pours out the love of God in our hearts (Romans 5:5), empowering us to serve other people. *Still, service, though important, is not central.*

MISSION: "HOW DO WE COMMUNICATE THE GOSPEL MESSAGE?"

The Book of Romans contains the clearest presentation of the gospel of Jesus. Martin Luther called Romans, "the most important document in the New Testament, the gospel in its purest expression."[3] Paul worked hard in his letter to the Romans to establish the truth and centrality of the gospel in contrast to Jewish thought and worship. Quoting from the Hebrew prophet Joel, Paul writes in Romans 10:13-14,

> *Everyone who calls on the name of the Lord will be saved. How, then, can they call on the one they have not believed in? And how can they believe in the one of whom they have not heard? And how can they hear without someone preaching to them?*

God has chosen us to be heralds proclaiming the power of his redeeming and transforming love.

Jesus' mission was to come find that which was lost, to restore that which was blind, to set free those who were held captive, and ultimately to resuscitate those who are dead. He carried out his plan in the most curious way. He came to rescue others by allowing himself to be killed. His death, and ultimate resurrection, became the very means of finding, rescuing, and healing. His life, death, and new life became the message by which his mission was—and is—accomplished. Surprisingly, he did not choose to proclaim the message through his resurrected body, but through his mystical body, the body of Christ, the Church. According to Paul, the Lord will rescue all those who call on him, if they hear the good news, if they believe, and if the good news is proclaimed through his followers. That is a series of big "ifs."

We have the awesome responsibility to rightly and effectively make known this wonderfully true story, the gospel—the death, burial, resurrection, and promised return of a king, the King of kings, King Jesus. We are called to use our creativity to proclaim the gospel to others in ways which are effective and culturally appropriate, but ultimately the ability to communicate the gospel comes from the Holy Spirit. Jesus told his original disciples to go into all the world and proclaim the gospel to everything that is breathing by preaching, teaching, and disciple-making. He promised to be with them. He gave them this directive to take his message to the nations of the world, but he told them, he *commanded* them, to wait in Jerusalem for power from on high. On the day of Pentecost after the resurrection of Jesus, the Holy Spirit descended and the early Christian community busted forth with evangelistic zeal, taking the gospel to the known world. The contemporary church has the same directive and the same enabling from the Holy Spirit. He empowers us to carry on the mission of Jesus, to take the gospel to every corner of the globe. *Still, mission, though important, is not central.*

COMMUNITY: "WHO ARE WE DOING LIFE WITH?"

The spiritual dimension of *doctrine* is what we believe in the Church. The spiritual dimensions of *ethics, devotion, service,* and *mission* are what we do in the Church, but *community* is who we are as a Church. The Church (upper case "C") includes the followers of Jesus spread around the world and those who have died in faith before us, but the church (lower case "c") is the local gathering of Christians. The idea that a person can be a Christian without being an integral part of a local church is completely foreign to the biblical writers and the historic Church. A rugged individualistic culture, as we see in the United States today, can easily define Christian spirituality in terms of a "*personal* relationship," or a "*personal* Lord and Savior," or an "*individual* encounter with the Holy Spirit," but an "individual Christian" is an oxymoron. There can only be community Christians.

The community of faith that Jesus is building in towns, cities, and villages all around the world is a "fellowship with the Spirit" (Philippians 2:1), a fellowship of the Spirit, a fellowship constructed by the Spirit. We are each an individual temple of the Holy Spirit and we each have individual responsibility to live a Spirit-empowered life of purity, but we are also a temple of the Holy Spirit collectively when we gather together.[4] We cannot simply claim to be the church all alone by ourselves. *How can an individual fulfill all of the "one another" commands if that individual is an isolated spiritual island? How can an individual love one another, care for one another, encourage one another, etc., when they are all alone?* The Spirit works to create local churches, local gatherings of Christians. The Spirit distributes his gifts for the building up of God's people in the local church. The community of faith is the Spirit's workshop, the canvas on which he paints his shape-shifting masterpiece. *Still, community, although exceedingly important, is not central.*

TRANSFORMATION: WHO ARE WE BECOMING?

Each of these spiritual dimensions is an inseparable component to Christian spirituality, but none of them can become the heart of Christian spirituality. They each draw their strength and life from the centrality of transformation. If *doctrine* becomes central, we face the temptation of making everything intellectual and becoming know-it-all Bible trivia experts who do nothing but lecture others with our superior knowledge. If *ethics* become central, we learn how to act right, but never learn to be right. This road leads to a legalistic form of spirituality that has no Spirit in it. If *devotion* becomes central, we have hearts full of emotionally-charged passion, but enthusiasm does little to rid us of sinful thoughts, motivations, and attitudes. If *service* becomes central, we contribute to the lives of people around us, but so easily fall into the trap of earning God's favor by our works. If *mission* is central, we go and proclaim, but do so from an empty heart and face the inevitability of burnout. If *community* becomes central, we construct beautiful buildings and fill them with activity, but in the end we become a self-sustained community that exists only for itself. We effectually become so inwardly focused that we turn living water into a tepid, putrid cesspool.

The center of Christian spirituality is spiritual transformation. The Holy Spirit is changing us to become people who know and understand right doctrine. He is changing us into the kind of people who do right, the kind of people who love Jesus with all of their hearts, the kind of people who desire to serve others. God himself through the Holy Spirit is shaping us to become the kind of people who live to proclaim the gospel and the kind of people who want to live in Christian community. Spiritual transformation is the shape-shifting spirituality of discipleship. In this reckless pursuit of God, transformation is the central spiritual dimension in our journey. We have to step back to the first spiritual dimension, doctrine, and ask ourselves, "What do we believe about God?" Spiritual transformation will become central, but it begins with discovering who this God of our pursuit is. To do this, we have to become theologians.

STUDY GUIDE

1. Have there been moments when the Spirit used the Scripture to guide you towards truth? Explain.

2. How has the Holy Spirit changed how you live your life? Has there ever been a moment of stark conviction causing you to re-evaluation the direction of your life? Explain.

3. How do you best express your devotion for God?

4. When was the last time you went out of your way to serve somebody without compensation or reward?

5. What is your greatest fear in sharing your faith? How can the Holy Spirit help conquer that fear?

6. Who are you the closest to in your local church? What drew you to these people?

7. Which of these six spiritual dimensions (doctrine, ethics, devotion, service, mission, or community) are you most likely to make central in your walk with the Holy Spirit?

8. Why must transformation remain the central focus of your spiritual life?

Chapter Three

REDISCOVERING GOD

*O Lord my God, my one hope, listen to me, for I fear that
through weariness I may be unwilling to seek You, but my
desire is "that I may always ardently seek Your face." Do
give me strength to seek you, who have made me find You,
and has given me the hope of finding You more and more.*

— AUGUSTINE —

I was really surprised the day someone told me I was a theologian. I was
sitting in a systematic theology class in seminary one day, when the professor announced to the entire class that we were all theologians. *What?
Me, a theologian?* When I heard the word "theologian," I thought of old,
bearded men wearing tweed jackets, biting on unlit pipes, and arguing
over how many angels can dance on the head of pin. I might have gone for
the beard and pipe, but certainly not the tweed jacket! *No,* I thought to
myself, *I am not a theologian—or am I?*

I soon learned that theologians were not the tweed-clad elderly
debaters of my imagination. We are all theologians. Anyone who has
a thought about God or who has come to the conclusion that such a
being does not exist is a theologian. Monotheists, pantheists, and athe-
ists are all making theological decisions. The question is not, "Are we
theologians?" Rather the question is "What kind of theologians are we
going to be?" Theology has gotten a bad reputation not because the art
of theological exploration is itself bad, but because too much pointless theology, passionless theology, and bad theology circles around the
life of the everyday Christian. The proliferation of bad theology is no
reason to ignore theological discussions. As fellow theologian Larry

Hart notes, "The answer to bad theology is not no theology, but good theology."[1]

Good theology is not the pointless pontificating in pursuit of correct doctrine. The work of good theology is the pursuit of God. It is not trying to understanding absolutely everything about the nature of God. Such a task is impossible. Theology works to discover God and understanding how his actions inter-relate with ours. Anselm, from the eleventh century, described theology as "faith seeking understanding." Theology is the journey of seeking the face of God. In theological pursuit, we do not study God as much as we study how God has revealed himself. God is not a subject to be studied. We cannot see him with a microscope or a telescope. We are completely dependent upon God to reveal himself to us. He has chosen to reveal himself through creation, his Son, the Scripture, and the faithful testimony of his Church. Theology as pursuit is not a special task for a select few, but is part of the normal Christian life.

At some point in time, most of us ask questions in pursuit of knowledge that is outside ourselves. When I think back to my childhood, I was always seeking to discover God. I remember on one occasion riding in the back seat of my parents' car and looking out the window and whispering the prayer, "God, if you are out there, can you make the trees sway?" We had stopped at a stop sign as I concluded my prayer. I looked up through the car window and, sure enough, the trees began to sway. Granted, this encounter was not the best evidence for the existence of God, but this prayer was a step in my theological journey. It was my early attempt at theological inquiry. Even at ten years old, I wanted to be a theologian. This prayer was my child-like faith seeking to discover an unseen presence I knew was out there.

SEEKING THE FACE OF THE HIDING GOD

King David, the warrior/poet and theologian, penned his passionate plea to worship God with singular devotion in Psalm 27. "One thing I ask of the LORD," he writes, "this is what I seek: that I may dwell in the house of the LORD all the days of my life, to gaze upon the beauty of the LORD and to seek him in his temple" (Psalm 27:4). Worshipping by gazing was not enough for David. He heard the call to seek the face of God, and he responded with resolve. He writes, "My heart says of you, 'Seek his face!' Your face, LORD, I will seek" (Psalm 27:8).

Christians for centuries have used the phrase "seeking the face of God" to describe their spiritual journey of discovering and rediscovering God in his glory. Augustine uses the phrase four times in his influential work *On the Trinity*, quoting from Psalm 105, "seek his face always."[2] Seeking the face of God is the worshipful rhythm of the pursuit of knowing, loving, and praising God. Augustine ends *On the Trinity* with a prayer:

> *...so far as I have been able, so far as You have made me to be able, I have sought You, and have desired to see with my understanding what I believed; and I have argued and labored much.*[3]

The goal of seeking God, according to Augustine, is not to increase our understanding, but to use the powers of understanding to see what we have believed, to discover the object of our devotion, to find God and see him in all of his goodness and greatness.

We must find him, because God has chosen to hide himself. He has chosen to cloak himself in mystery. Skeptics and critics of the Christian faith often ask, "Why hasn't God made himself more obvious?" Good question. It would seem that God would make himself more prominent if indeed he desires to have a relationship with us, but God hides from our human eyes on purpose. He wants us to enjoy the adventure of finding him. He wants us to feel the joy of anticipation much like kids playing hide and seek. I loved playing hide and seek as a kid. I was a rather lanky and skinny child, which made hiding easy for me. I was all arms and legs, but I could fold myself up and hide in some of the best places.

I enjoyed playing hide and seek as a child, but I enjoy playing hide and seek as a father so much more. When my boys were younger, I loved to hide from them and pop out in inopportune moments. Very often they would respond with a shriek of laughter. The fondest memories of playing hide and seek with my boys were the times when I would hide and my oldest son, Wesley, would be seeking. I would find the best hiding place, and he would count to twenty. As he darted out throughout the house to find me, I would hear his little footsteps loudly closing in on my position. I would remain perfectly still and wait for him to pass. Then I would make some kind of noise or rattle the furniture to get his attention. *I really wanted him to find me.* He would run back and began to shout, "Daddy, where are you!" I would try to hold back my laughter and wait a moment until he had turned to look somewhere else, and I would jump up and yell. He would flash a look of complete fear, and then we would bust out laughing.

I could have remained hidden, but I wanted him to find me. The excitement is in the discovery, but the degree of excitement depends upon the anticipation. If I were to hide in the same room where he was counting with eyes closed, there would be little anticipation. If I hid right out in the open, then there would be no anticipation and no excitement in the discovery. God has called us to an eternal and cosmic game of hide and seek. He has hidden himself away, and he has called for us to come and seek his face, to discover him for who he really is.

As I have devoted my life to this game of hide and seek, the journey of discovering the One who made me, I have found it helpful to allow my search to be guided by two words: *holy* and *love*. These two words express the nature of God in a complete way.[4] *Who is God? What can we say about him?* He is holy love. These two qualities work together and complement each other. The path to bad theology begins by taking a step towards one of these concepts to the exclusion of the other. If people only see God's holiness, they will be led down a path that will distort their picture of God. They will begin to form images of God who is nothing more than the Grinch, a grouchy, vindictive, angry little man with a heart that is two sizes too small. If people only see God's loveliness, they will have a different, but equally warped, view of God. They will begin to see a God who is nothing more than a giant Santa Claus in the sky surrounded by sunflowers, rainbows and cute, little bunny rabbits. God is not only holy. God is not only love. He is both. He is holy love.

THE HOLINESS OF GOD

Conversations about holiness among Christians inevitably end up in a discussion about rules and regulations, long lists of what we *cannot do* as followers of Christ. Contemporary concepts of holiness too often imply participation in certain rituals, devotional practices, corporate worship services, small group Bible studies, and other religious activities, as well as keeping certain regulations which vary from one Christian tradition to another. Regulations range from rules regarding food, drink, dress, and social relationships to worship practices, choice of vocabulary, and appropriate sources entertainment. These images of holiness promote a vague impression of the holiness of God. It portrays the holiness of God in terms of a God who prescribes certain rituals and mandates certain regulations. In the times before Jesus, God did prescribe a detailed list of rituals whereby people could worship the living God. He gave the *torah* (the law) to instruct people how to live a life pleasing to him. We can see glimpses of the nature of God and his relationship with humanity in these rituals and regulations, but they do not adequately paint the picture of his holiness. This picture of holiness is better painted by the prophets/poets and the songwriters of the Scripture.

Moses, who is known as the law-giver, was also a songwriter. After God rescued his people from the encroaching Egyptian army by parting the Red Sea, Moses wrote a song, celebrating their Rescuer. Midway through the song, Moses declares, "Who among the gods is like you, O LORD? Who is like you—majestic in holiness, awesome in glory, working wonders?" (Exodus 15:11)

Moses' poetic picture of God is the one who is "majestic in holiness." Those of us who have grown up in the United States have little experiential knowledge of "majesty." If you listen to the average American in conversation, I doubt you will ever hear them use the word "majestic." The Hebrew word for "majestic" means "to be great, wise, noble."[5] To call people majestic is to say they carry themselves with nobility. In American culture we have lost the concept of nobility. As we define ourselves in purely subjective, individualistic terms there is no sense of nobility—no concept that a certain set of character traits is greater or more preferable than others. We all become equal as we define ourselves by our own private standards. When we lose the concept of nobility among ourselves, we have trouble understanding God who is holy.

To call God holy does not mean he is religious, as defined by rules and ritual. Certainly God has made himself known by his law, but the law in itself is not what makes God holy. The law was given as our tutor, showing us our sin. To call God *holy* or to sing of the God who is "majestic in holiness" as Moses did, is to say that God is separate, different, and altogether other than his creation. He is not a common run-of-the-mill kind of deity. He is sacred. Humanity cannot find an adequate comparison when we choose language to talk about God. He is too big, too grand, too massive for us to ever completely wrap our minds around all he is. Isaiah makes the point with the cadence and rhythm of an old-time, holiness evangelist:

To whom, then, will you compare God? What image will you com-
pare him to? As for an idol, a craftsman casts it, and a gold-
smith overlays it with gold and fashions silver chains for it.
A man too poor to present such an offering selects wood that
will not rot.
He looks for a skilled craftsman to set up an idol that will not
topple.
Do you not know?
Have you not heard?
Has it not been told you from the beginning?
Have you not understood since the earth was founded?
He sits enthroned above the circle of the earth, and its people are
like grasshoppers.
He stretches out the heavens like a canopy,
And spreads them out like a tent to live in. (Isaiah 40:18-22)

What an incredibly awesome and holy God! One cannot read texts like this one from Isaiah without wrestling with the grandeur of God.

In the absence of this holy vision of God, people create in their own image a lesser god, an impotent god, a small god who is not compatible with contemporary life. J.B. Phillips notes that a "small god" concept in some people leads to an inner dissatisfaction. He kindly notes that people are not discontented because they are merely wicked and rebellious:

...but because they have not found with their adult minds a God
big enough to 'account for' life, big enough to 'fit in with' the new
scientific age, big enough to command their highest admiration and
respect, and consequently their willing cooperation.[6]

God is bigger than the biggest object we can imagine with our finite minds. His bigness is an inseparable component of his holiness.

THE LOVELINESS OF GOD

In contrast to his holiness is his loveliness. God is lovely in one sense in that he is the perfection of beauty. The 18th century Catholic hymn writer, Alphonsus Liguori, wrote:

O God of loveliness, O Lord of Heaven above,
How worthy to possess my heart's devoted love.

So sweet Thy countenance, so gracious to behold
That one, one only glance to me were bliss untold.

David describes his desire to "gaze upon the beauty of the LORD" (Psalm 27:4). In our church, we still sing "*O Lord you're beautiful, your face is all we seek.*" God is lovely to gaze upon with eyes tightly shut. To stand in his presence with an open heart and open hands and to worship him in the beauty of holiness is to see his loveliness. His beauty does not tarnish or wrinkle. It is a creative beauty that does not change or diminish. He is the originator of all that we understand to be beautiful.

He is lovely in his ongoing act of creation, but the loveliness of God extends beyond the sweetness of his countenance. He is not only lovely; he is love. To see God's loveliness is to see that he is, by nature, love. The love that we express in our human relationships reflects, in a limited form, this essential quality of God. John writes, "Whoever does not love does not know God, because God is love" (1 John 4:8). Everything we express and know to be true about love is a mere imprint of God's nature. In his instructions on the use of spiritual gifts in the context of community worship, Paul celebrates the necessity of love. People can speak in tongues, speak prophetic poetry, understand the deep things of God, and have the faith to move a behemoth-sized mountain, but if they do not possess love, they are nothing.[7] Love is the way we demonstrate our creation in God's image. He made us to be people of love, because he himself is a God of love. The love we experience in human relationships is a mere shadow of the greatness and brightness of God's love. His love has a depth and width and length we can explore but will never exhaust.

We can see God's love in his story of redemption recorded in the Old Testament and the New Testament. The law was given through Moses, and grace and truth came in living form in Jesus, but God's love spanned the two testaments. A shallow reading of the Scriptures has led some to conclude falsely that there are two different gods described in the two testaments. They wrongly assume that the God in the Old Testament is a God of judgment—an angry, maniacal dictator who is ready to execute his justice in forms of lighting bolts upon unsuspecting sinners—and the God of the New Testament is a peace-loving, sunflower in the sky, poised to rain buckets of blessings upon his creation.[8] Both images are caricatures of the one true God who demonstrated his heart of love in both testaments. God declared his love in the Old Testament:

- *God loved Abraham with a steadfast and faithful love. (Genesis 24:27)*

- *God loved Jacob and chose him over Esau. (Malachi 1:2)*

- *God loved Joseph even while Joseph was in prison. (Genesis 39:21)*

- *God loved David with a love that would not depart. (2 Samuel 7:15; 22:51; 1 Chronicles 17:13; 2 Chronicles 1:8; 6:42; Isaiah 55:3)*

- *God loved Job in his time of physical suffering. (Job 10:12)*

- *God loved Hezekiah in his time of physical restoration. (Isaiah 38:17)*

- *God expressed his love to Daniel in a vision. (Daniel 10:11)*

Without question, the Old Testament reveals how God loved Israel. He loved Israel with lovingkindness, with a steadfast love. The Hebrew word for this kind of love is *hesed*, which is found more than 200 times in the Old Testament. It speaks of God's covenant love, his everlasting love, a love that found its fullest expression in the death, burial, and resurrection of Jesus.

UNITED IN MYSTERY

The holiness and the loveliness of God are two inseparable and yet seemingly contradictory qualities. When we see God do something out of his holiness such as acts of wrath and anger, we often question how he can still be loving. When we observe God doing something out of his loveliness, such as forgiving sinners who are undeserving, we question how he can still be holy. These two qualities are united together in a mysterious relationship. A holy God of love defies simplistic descriptions. He is not merely a holy God of anger, wrath, judgment and justice. Neither is he a God of love filled with compassion, mercy, grace, and kindness. He is both holy and love simultaneously. Such mysterious depth caused Paul to exclaim:

Oh, the depth of the riches of the wisdom and knowledge of God! How unsearchable his judgments, and his paths beyond tracing out!

*"Who has known the mind of the Lord? Or who has been his coun-
selor?" "Who has ever given to God, that God should repay him?"
For from him and through him and to him are all things. To him be
the glory forever! Amen. (Romans 11:33-36)*

To remove the element of mystery from any descriptions of God is
to cease describing the God of the Christian community—the God worshipped, served, and proclaimed by Christians for centuries.

The temptation of the relevance-obsessed, contemporary church is
to remove all of the mystery out of God in order to make God easier
to approach. Evangelical churches in particular face this temptation of
relevance, reducing God's holiness in order to make him seem more appealing to those outside the faith. The temptation to reduce God's holiness
typically begins with a consideration of the thoughts of non-Christians.
*Will they want to come to our local church if we talk about this mysteri-
ous God of holy love?* Donald McCullough describes this temptation as
trivializing God. He writes,

> *We prefer the illusion of a safer deity, and so we have pared God
> down to more manageable proportions. Our era has no exclusive
> claim to the trivialization of God. This has always been the tempta-
> tion and the failure for the people of God. Pagan gods have caused
> less trouble than the tendency to re-fashion God into a more conge-
> nial, serviceable god.*[9]

A God without mystery becomes a god whom we completely understand, measure, predict, and ultimately control. Our God cannot and will
not be controlled by anyone. He is holy. He is love. He is a mystery.

STUDY GUIDE

1. What were your childhood images of God? How did they change as you grew up?

2. If you, like King David, could ask one thing of the Lord, what would it be?

3. Recall one time in your life when it seemed God was only holy, and one time when he was only loving. How did this perception impact your faith?

4. What would your spiritual journey be like if God was only holy?

5. What would your spiritual journey be like if God was only love?

6. Where in Scripture do we see God's holiness and loveliness displayed simultaneously?

7. When have you experienced both God's holiness and loveliness in the same occasion in your life?

8. What needs to change in your life to free you up to rediscover God?

Chapter Four

THE KINGDOM OF SELF

My child, be not a murmurer, since it leads the way to blasphemy. Be neither self-willed nor evil-minded, for out of all these blasphemies are engendered. Rather, be meek, since the meek shall inherit the earth. Be long-suffering and pitiful and guileless and gentle and good and always trembling at the words which you have heard. You shall not exalt yourself, nor give over-confidence to your soul.

— THE DIDACHE —

A dark kingdom stands in direct opposition to this wonderfully divine discovery of our mysterious God. Jesus proclaimed the presence of God's kingdom and taught us to pray for God's kingdom to come. The kingdom of God is not a place but a power. God rules and reigns over the earth from his kingdom. The Old Testament speaks of God's throne, because he reigns from a certain position. The Psalmist writes, "The LORD has established his throne in heaven, and his kingdom rules over all" (Psalm 103:19). The essence of God's kingdom can be described with two words: authority and obedience.

The kingdom of God comes when God is in the position of ultimate authority and we willingly obey. The kingdom of God is like teaching a teenager to drive. I dread the day I have to teach my boys to drive. I have never had the blessed opportunity to teach a teenager to operate a motor vehicle, but during my years as a youth pastor, I rode with a select few teenagers who were learning to drive. If you have a problem maintaining a disciplined life of prayer, let me encourage you to ride with a fifteen or sixteen-year-old who is just learning to drive. I promise you it will increase your prayer life! It is an opportunity to test your faith every time you buckle up with a teenager at the wheel.

On a few occasions I let teenagers drive my vehicle or I rode with them in theirs. What I learned in these rare moments of insanity was that only one person can hold the steering wheel. We teach teens to drive with two hands at the wheel, one at the ten o'clock position and the other at the two o'clock position. With their hands safely at "ten" and "two," they are in the best position to operate the motor vehicle safely (emphasis on "safely"). There is only one steering wheel, and only the driver can hold it. There is also only one brake pedal, although some parents think they have an invisible brake pedal on the passenger floorboard that they can stomp at any time. One of the worst scenarios when you are riding with a teenager behind the wheel would be to grab the wheel and try to steer. If two people try to steer at the same time, it will always end up in disaster.

Only one person can steer your life. Only one person can be in control of your life. You have entered the kingdom of God when God has authority over you, when he is the ultimate boss. If you grew up with older siblings, you may have been a broken record saying, "You're not the boss of me!" Nevertheless, somebody is going to be the boss of your life. It may be a friend, a parent, a relative, a spouse, a child, and just maybe, yourself. Somebody has to be the one calling the shots and making the decisions. When you receive the kingdom of God, you hand him the keys, move out of the driver's seat and let God take the wheel. You have entered his kingdom when God rules and reigns over your heart.

Kingdoms are made for a variety of reasons, but one of the main purposes is battle. Kingdoms were made for war. Kingdoms have always been involved in battles, whether morally good or bad. God's kingdom has been engaged in a battle since the Garden of Eden. The primary enemy to the kingdom of God may be rather unexpected. *Which kingdom is the number one enemy to the kingdom of God?* Most people answer "the kingdom of Satan" or "the kingdom of darkness." I understand why that answer is our natural response. We have grown up in a world of good guys and bad guys where the good guy wears a white hat and the bad guy wears a black hat. Every Luke Skywalker has a Darth Vader. Every Superman has a Lex Luther. I am not surprised to find most people rushing to identify the kingdom of Satan as the enemy to the kingdom of God, but the enemy to God's kingdom is much more seductive, much more seditious. The true enemy of the kingdom of God and the real barrier to discovering God is the kingdom of self.

The devil and the "spiritual forces of evil in the heavenly realms" are very real enemies to the kingdom of God (Ephesians 6:12). At the root of the devil's demise was his decision to align himself with the kingdom of self rather than the kingdom of God. Historically, the church has looked to Isaiah 14:12-14 as insight into the devil's rebellion:

> *How you have fallen from heaven, O morning star, son of the dawn! You have been cast down to the earth, you who once laid low the nations! You said in your heart, "I will ascend to heaven; I will raise my throne above the stars of God; I will sit enthroned on the mount of assembly, on the utmost heights of the sacred mountain. I will ascend above the tops of the clouds; I will make myself like the Most High. (Isaiah 14:12-14)*

This passage has caused some confusion because the phrase "O morning star" is translated "Lucifer" in the King James Version. This translation has led some to believe that the devil's name was Lucifer before he rebelled and it was changed to Satan after he rebelled.[1] The Scripture never records God changing Satan's name, but he certainly removed Satan from his privileged position in heaven.

In its historical context, the morning star of Isaiah 14:12 may have referred to one of the kings of Babylon. Since the days of the early church, Christians have interpreted this verse as both a reference to an earthly king and a reference to Satan's downfall.[2] I agree with the church fathers that while this verse originally spoke of a Babylonian king, it is also a reference to the devil. Jesus said he saw Satan falling like lightning from heaven.[3] Jesus' comment gives a bit of clarity to the Isaiah 14:12 reference to the morning star. The Bible does not say "Lucifer" was his name before he rebelled and was expelled from heaven. He rebelled because he chose to align himself with the kingdom of self. According to Isaiah, he said "I will" five times:

> *I will ascend to heaven.*
> *I will raise my throne above the stars of God.*
> *I will sit enthroned on the mount of assembly...*

I will ascend above the tops of the clouds.
I will make myself like the Most High.

The kingdom of the devil is fueled by the kingdom of self—the true culprit and opponent to the kingdom of God. Self is the true enemy.

When I was in Boy Scouts during junior high, we used to go on monthly camping trips. During one trip, we were dropped off outside a state park and given a map. We were shown where we were on the map and where we needed to go. We strapped our backpacks on our backs and headed out. When you have to go from point A to point B across unfamiliar terrain, it is helpful to have a map. However, it will do you no good if you cannot point the map in the direction you need to go. You need a compass to get your map pointed in the same direction that you are looking. We were able to reach our destination after hours of hiking, but we had to continue to stop and reorient the map to the compass reading.[4] The kingdom of self is like a compass orienting our hearts toward the desires of self. Life is from self and for self. The kingdom of God is oriented around the desires of God. Life is from God and for God.

These two kingdoms are actively in a head-to-head conflict with each other. Jesus said the kingdom of God was within us.[5] The kingdom of God belongs to the Father. It is his kingdom and he has made Jesus both Lord and King. The Holy Spirit is the executor of that kingdom making the kingdom real within our hearts. He is establishing God's rule and producing God's fruit within us. The Holy Spirit establishes God's kingly rule while facing continual opposition from the kingdom of self. The self works hard to establish its kingdom within our hearts with self as the king and executor. These two are in constant conflict. Paul used the Greek word *sarx*, translated "flesh" or "sinful nature," to describe the kingdom of self. Consider some of the references Paul makes to the self. Paul wrote, "For the sinful nature (*the self*) desires what is contrary to the Spirit, and the Spirit what is contrary to the sinful nature (*the self*). They are in conflict with each other, so that you do not do what you want" (Galatians 5:17).

There is a self within Paul, an old self, who has not been redeemed, and it is somehow separate from the new self who controls his will. It sounds like Paul needs some serious therapy, but he is speaking authentically about his struggle with the kingdom of self. Paul writes of his battle with sheer honesty: "I (*in the kingdom of self*) have been crucified with

Christ and I (*in the kingdom of self*) no longer live, but Christ lives in me. The life I live in the body, I (*in the kingdom of God*) live by faith in the Son of God, who loved me and gave himself for me" (Galatians 2:20).

This picture of the kingdom of self at war with the kingdom of God within us helps in understanding Romans 7:15-20. The interpretation of this passage has been a historic debate among Bible scholars and commentators. Some understand Paul to be speaking about his situation before coming to Christ. Others see Romans 7 as Paul's present struggle after coming to Christ.[6] I believe Paul is writing about his present struggle. He writes in the first person using the present, progressive tense, because he is describing the ongoing battle between the kingdom of God and the kingdom of self. Let me take some liberty and rewrite the Romans 7:15-20 using the imagery of the kingdom of self:

> *I do not understand what self does. For what I want to do self does not do, but what I hate self does. And if self does what I do not want to do, I agree that the law is good. As it is, it is no longer I myself who do it, but it is sin living in me. I know that nothing good lives in me, that is, in my sinful nature. For I have the desire to do what is good, but self cannot carry it out. For what self does is not the good I want to do; no, the evil I do not want to do—this self keeps on doing. Now if self does what I do not want to do, it is no longer I who do it, but it is sin living in me that does it.*

It is the Holy Spirit who establishes the kingdom of God in our hearts by producing fruit—certain character traits—within us. The Spirit engages in a battle against the dreaded kingdom of self in order to establish the kingdom of God. I am not the warrior in this battle. I am the object. The Spirit is battling for supremacy over our hearts.

The Spirit is battling the self, but "self" is a complex issue. Jesus commented on the kingdom of self when talking to his disciples. He said, "For whoever wants to save his life will lose it, but whoever loses his life for me will save it. What good is it for a man to gain the whole world, and yet lose or forfeit his very self?" (Luke 9:24-25) The word "self" is a reflexive pronoun referring back to "life." A person's self is his or her life. The Greek word translated "life" is the word *psuche*, meaning "the breath of life" or "immortal soul."

There are different ways to divide up the human self. One of the more popular ways is to divide up the human person into three parts—body, soul, and spirit. The popular catch phrase is that the human person is a spirit who has a soul and lives in a body. While this three-part division is plausible, this common catch phrase tends to devalue the body and is not the best explanation of the human person. The most basic way to look at the complexities of the human self is in divide it into two categories: the body and the soul, the outer self and the inner self. The inner self is the self that Jesus does not want people to forfeit.

Some Christians are under the impression that the self must be obliterated. These Christians try to "hide in the shadow of the cross." They claim self must diminish until it loses its shape and voice and ultimately becomes extinct. They do not to become shape shifters but shape obliterators. The annihilation of the self is not the nature of the kingdom of God. The Triune God never intends for our selves to fade away. Jesus said he did not want us to forfeit or lose our self. The kingdom of God is opposed to the kingdom of self, where life is oriented around self—where life is from self and for self. Self does not need to be destroyed; it needs to be deconstructed, taken apart, and placed in submission to the kingdom of God. This process of deconstruction is both necessary and difficult if we are to become true, biblical shape shifters. It is necessary according to Jesus' request, and it is difficult because we live in a self-perpetuating world.

One day as I was reflecting on this obsession with self, I hammered out the following playful and purposefully redundant bit of prose:

Our world is self-absorbed with self-acceptance and will continue the search for self-actualization until our self-aggrandizing lifestyle of self-appointed self-care leaves us completely self-centered. If we do not start a process of self-cleaning our self-consumed heart, we will end up self-defeated and self-deprecating drones. Any kind of self-deluded self-description that is self-directed will result in a self-disgusted self-display of self-education. Why do we cling to thoughts of self-existence that only creates self-hating instead of self-imposed self-improvement? A self-initiated pursuit of self-obsession is inherently self-ordained but the underling evil is in the self-orientation. The self-pleasing life that is self-preoccupied will never be self-preserving even though it is self-produced. A self-professed heart may be self-promoted, but it can never be self-protective. In the end, self-worship robs us of our very selves.

A preoccupation with the self is the essence of the kingdom of self. It robs us of our true identities, preventing us from becoming the people God created us and designed us to be. God's plan to transform us into the image of his Son by the Holy Spirit makes us more ourselves, more human, the kind of persons he desires for us to be. The roadblock to this work in the Church is the kingdom of self fueled by a consumer-driven form of Christianity, a form of the Christian life focused on meeting the needs of people. The kingdom of self as a present day form of evil can be alive and well within local churches where people believe their blessing and benefit is the highest good.

It is not surprising to see the kingdom of self building such a stronghold in our lives, because we (in the West) live in a world that has been shaped by one statement from Rene Descartes, a French philosopher from the seventeenth century. Descartes went on a philosophical journey of doubt. He wanted to work through everything he knew and could possibly doubt until he could locate a philosophical foundation where he could doubt no more. He came up with one statement, a statement that changed the course of Western civilization. The one statement was, in Latin, *cogito ergo sum*—I think, therefore I am. For Descartes, all knowledge could be reduced down to one certain truth—I know that I exist because I am a thinking person. This statement shaped the Enlightenment, the cultural shift of eighteenth-century Europe, where reason became dominant over tradition, religious sensibilities, and mythology. The predominance of reason was the triumph of the kingdom of self. Upon this foundation, the self becomes the focal point of reality. The active belief in the autonomous, sovereign, thinking self is at the heart of the kingdom of self.

The kingdom of self begins as a self-orientation, which is problematic, but worse than a wrong orientation is the kingdom of self's tendency to worship itself. When we make a god of our own hearts, we create a contemporary form of idol worship. Typically, Christians in the West see idol worship as a phenomenon only in Eastern religions. They think only of Hindus bowing and bringing offerings to shining icons in brightly colored temples. Idol worship is not just devotion given to an object. We can easily make our own lives an idol and mask our own deceit by calling it "self-actualization" or "following our dreams." An idol is anything (or anyone) we worship instead of the one true living God. In the United States, there is no more prevalent idol than the idol of self. G.K. Chesterton writes,

> *An unselfish egoist is a man who has pride without the excuse of passion. Of all conceivable forms of enlightenment the worst is what these people call the Inner Light. Of all horrible religions the most horrible is the worship of the god within.*[7]

People within an individualist, modern culture have difficulty seeing the seduction of the kingdom of self. We can easily wrap the god of self in biblical language and convince ourselves that obsession with personal benefit (as we determine what is beneficial) is not self worship, but merely our living in God's blessings. The Scripture does make promises for us to receive, but these blessings are always means towards the greater end of loving God and loving people.

The kingdom of self is the biggest obstacle to discovering who God has revealed himself to be and how to live in a dynamic, shape-shifting process of spiritual transformation. The kingdom of self says, "I exist, because I am a thinking autonomous self." The kingdom of God says, "I exist because I was created for God and by God." We are born into the kingdom of self. We come into the world kicking and screaming, declaring to the world, "I want. I need. I feel." Eugene Peterson refers to this as the replacement trinity—an "unholy trinity of Holy Wants, Holy Needs, and Holy Feelings."[8] When we deconstruct self and submit it to the kingdom of God, we begin to discover God who is holy love. Nowhere is God's mysterious nature of holy love better demonstrated than in the doctrine of the Trinity, the authentic Trinity, the ancient Christian doctrine concerning the nature of the one living God who has revealed himself in three persons—the Father, Son and Holy Spirit.

STUDY GUIDE

1. What would a life lived fully in *the kingdom of self* look like?

2. What would a life lived fully in *the kingdom of God* look like?

3. When have you felt the battle between the kingdom of God and the kingdom of self waging war in your heart?

4. What typically prevents people from giving control of their lives to King Jesus?

5. What area of your life is the most difficult to submit to God?

6. How have you experienced consumer-driven Christianity? What has been your reaction?

7. How do we respectfully receive God's blessings without turning them into ammunition for the kingdom of self?

Chapter Five

WHY I AM A TRINITARIAN CHRISTIAN: THEOLOGICAL REASONS

All are of One, by unity (that is) of substance; while the mystery of the dispensation is still guarded, which distributes the Unity into a Trinity, placing in their order the three Persons—the Father, the Son, and the Holy Spirit: three, however, not in condition, but in degree; not in substance, but in form; not in power, but in aspect; yet of one substance, and of one condition, and of one power, inasmuch as He is one God.

— TERTULLIAN —

Understanding God as three-in-one has become more than a mere intellectual doctrine in my spiritual journey; it has become an invigorating adventure. I remember the first analogy I heard trying to describe the mystery of the Trinity. I was a teenager and a young believer eager to soak up all my local church and the Scriptures had to teach. I was listening to a Christian comedian on my Walkman by way of cassette tape. He was talking about how easy it is to understand the Trinity—as easy as pie, in fact. He described in vivid terms a really good, homemade cherry pie, the kind of pie that would spill the filling out of each side when you tried to put a slice on your plate. He said to imagine taking that cherry pie and cutting it into three equal pieces. The knife would penetrate through the flaky crust on top clear through the gooey center into the bottom crust. When the knife was removed, the center would all ooze back together, but the crust would reveal three clear lines of demarcation. "This cherry pie," he remarked with confidence, "is a picture of the Trinity." According to this illustration, there is one God represented by the one pie filling and three persons—the Father, Son and Holy Spirit—that appear to be three different persons. This creative description of the Trinity did not really help me understand how three can equal one. All that his colorful description did was make me hungry for cherry pie!

Countless analogies have been used to try to describe how God can be three and one at the same time. All of them fail. All human illustrations break down at some point. Whether it is the cherry pie illustration, the ice-water-vapor illustration or the baseball team illustration, they all fall short of actually describing how the Father, the Son, and the Holy Spirit are three different persons of the one God. I have all but given up on using analogies to resolve the logical contradiction inherit in the Trinity, but out of necessity I do use one or two illustrations to invite people to discover the three-in-one nature of the God they love, worship, and serve. The illustrations are imperfect, but they do help people wrestle with this mystery.

One illustration I use is a personal one. I am a pastor. When I am teaching most people know me as a pastor and teacher. This context is a great way to get to know me, because so much of my personally is revealed in my teaching. People can see both my serious pursuit of God in the context of historical theology and my light-heartedness (and at times silly) through my never-ending reflections on popular culture. Nevertheless, I am not only Pastor Derek, I am also Moopy. If people want to know me they have to know me as Moopy as well as Pastor. "Moopy" is the playful name I am called by my wife. It is a shortened form of the name "Shmoopy" from "The Soup Nazi," one of the most popular episodes of 1990's TV sitcom, *Seinfeld*.[1] I am not only a pastor and Moopy, but I am Daddy. I have two boys, and after the birth of my firstborn son, my identity changed. I became Wesley's dad. A person could say they know me well because they have heard me teach, but pastor/teacher is not me in totality. If you only know me as pastor and you don't know me as Moopy or Daddy, then you don't know me fully.

Similarly, if we want to know God fully we cannot know him as Jesus only, which is the temptation of some evangelicals. We cannot know God fully if we know him only as the Holy Spirit, a temptation of some charismatics. We cannot know God fully as Father, the temptation of some nominal Christians. To know God for who he is, to know God in the richness of his personhood, we have to experience him as Father, Son, and Holy Spirit. My illustration is not an attempt to explain the nature of the triune God. In my illustration I am one person in three roles. At this point my illustration breaks down. The Triune God is not one God in three roles or modes; this concept is the heresy of modalism.[2] God is one in nature, in divine substance, who has revealed himself in three persons. In my flawed illustration, I want to encourage people to discover God for all he is without ending our search one-third or two-thirds of the way.

Rediscovering God as the Trinity—as the Father, Son, and Holy Spirit—has catapulted my spiritual walk forward. It has connected me with fellow God-seekers in my generation and those who have lived long ago. My exploration of the triune God has given me a perspective on life, ministry, and spiritual formation that is overtly Trinitarian. It has shaped my identity. I have become intentionally a Trinitarian Christian. I am commonly asked, "*Why is the doctrine of the Trinity so important to you?*" As I have thought, prayed, studied, discussed, and taught on the Trinity over the years, I have come to seven thoughtful answers to that question. Why is the Trinity so important? Here is my reply:

1. *The Bible reveals God as three-in-one.*

2. *The historical, orthodox, Christian Church confesses a triune God.*

3. *The doctrine of the Trinity holds together all we believe.*

4. *The love expressed in the Trinity draws me into a community.*

5. *The triune nature of God underscores the value of relationships.*

6. *The mystery displayed in the Trinity demands my worship.*

7. *Three dominant Christian traditions correspond to the persons of the Trinity.*

The first three statements are more theological reasons, and the last four are more practical reasons why I believe the doctrine of the Trinity is so vital to our Christian lives. These seven reasons are why I have intentionally become a Trinitarian Christian.

THE BIBLE REVEALS GOD AS THREE-IN-ONE

The Scriptures, composed of both the Old Testament and the New Testament, are the central text in the Christian faith. While there are segments of the intellectual community that question its authenticity and uniqueness, the Bible remains firmly planted in the world-wide and heavenly community Jesus is building. Since the early days of the Christian movement, the Scriptures made up of the Torah, the prophets, the psalms and wisdom literature, the gospels, the teachings and acts of the apostles, and the apocalyptic revelation of John have been regarded as the highest authority in matters of faith. They serve as the one, unique, God-breathed script by which we see, know, and worship the one living God.

Some in the Christian community would say, *"Since God is one, why can't we just follow Jesus? Why all of this confusing talk about the Trinity? The Bible doesn't use the word 'Trinity' anyway. Can't we just simply follow Jesus?"* Darrell Johnson describes a simple relationship with Jesus that leads us to the Trinity. He writes, "It is precisely when we do focus on the simple facts of Jesus that we find ourselves drawn into theological grappling which keeps ending up at the doctrine of the Trinity."[3] In the Old Testament it is easy to see the oneness of God. Yahweh is the God of Israel and there are no other gods before him. He is the one, true living God. The coming of Jesus reveals the threeness of God. In God's transcendence, he displays his holiness, and we see that he is one. In the incarnation, God displays the loving act of giving his one and only Son. And through the Son, God sends the Holy Spirit to glorify the Son. In the incarnation of Jesus and the coming of the Holy Spirit, we see that God is three.

The Scripture testifies that Jesus was worshipped as the Son of God. People worshiped him at his birth. Soon after he was born, perhaps even years after his birth, wise men came from the east, and when they saw Jesus with his mother they "fell down and worshiped him" (Matthew 2:11). When Jesus grew up and became a man, he started an itinerate ministry preaching the gospel, teaching the things of the kingdom of God, healing the sick, and gathering together a small community of followers. His closest twelve followers, his disciples, grew to worship him as the Son of God. On one occasion they were rowing across the Galilean Sea at night when a storm blew in over the water. The wind and waves sought to capsize the boat. As the night grew late and the wind blew harder, they saw a figure walking on the water. It was Jesus. When he entered the boat, the wind ceased and the Bible says, "Those in the boat worshiped him, saying, 'Truly you are the Son of God'" (Matthew 14:33). After the resurrection, when Jesus had conquered death itself, eleven of his disciples saw him on a mountain in Galilee, and there they worshipped him (Matthew 28:17). The Scripture clearly portrays Jesus as God, the one true God whom his Jewish followers worship.

As his modern-day followers, we too worship Jesus as God. We pray to Jesus. We sing songs to Jesus. We talk about Jesus. We confess our sins to Jesus. We teach our children about Jesus. We preach Jesus crucified, buried, and risen from the dead. When we draw near to Jesus in simple devotion, we begin to see images of the Trinity. As we pay close attention to his teachings, we hear him calling God his father. At one point Jesus tells a group of Jewish leaders, "If I glorify myself, my glory is nothing. It is my Father who glorifies me, of whom you say, 'He is our God'" (John 8:54). He had the audacity to call God *his Father*, a scandalous act for the Jews. They were ready to stone him for an apparently flippant comment.

As we continue to follow Jesus, we also hear him talking about the Holy Spirit. He says, "But the Helper, the Holy Spirit, whom the Father will send in my name, he will teach you all things and bring to your remembrance all that I have said to you" (John 14:26). Now we have a bigger problem. We have gone from "The LORD our God, the LORD is one" to God as a Father having a Son and sending a spirit, his Spirit, in the name of his Son. *How are we to resolve the tension between the oneness of God and the variety we see in the nature of God through Jesus' own words?* The great discovery made by the Church is the discovery of the Trinity. The word "Trinity" is not used in any of these Scripture references (or anywhere else in the Bible for that matter). It is the word we use to describe these three persons who all seem to be God.

The doctrine of the Trinity helps us to know God in his fullness as Father, Son, and Holy Spirit and worship him as the one and only God. As followers of Jesus we embrace what the Scriptures teach. We work to bring people into a relationship with this triune God. When the disciples worshiped Jesus after his resurrection, Jesus spoke to them and said, "All authority in heaven and on earth has been given to me. Go therefore and make disciples of all nations, baptizing them in the name of the Father and of the Son and of the Holy Spirit..." (Matthew 28:18-19). He instructed his original disciples, and us who are his present disciples, to baptize people in the name, the one singular name—God the Father, the Son, and the Holy Spirit. The preposition translated "in" is the Greek word *eis* meaning "into." He does not merely call us to baptize people in the authority of his name. He is calling us to baptize people *into* the triune name, into a loving and eternal relationship with the Triune God, a God who is one God revealed as Father, Son, and Holy Spirit.

THE HISTORICAL, ORTHODOX, CHRISTIAN CHURCH CONFESSES A TRIUNE GOD

The term "Trinity" (*trinitas* in Latin) was coined by Tertullian in the third century to express the reality that God is one, but God is not alone. The Church did not invent the doctrine of the Trinity to solve the mystery of the one God and the three persons revealed in the Scriptures to be God. The Church began to use the term to clarify what it had always believed. The New Testament speaks of the Father, Son, and Holy Spirit in various portions of Scripture.[4] The clearest and most undeniable reference to the Trinity is in Matthew 19 when Jesus calls his disciples to baptize, to immerse, people into the triune name of God.

Historically, the Father, Son, and Holy Spirit were worshiped as the one God of the Christian Church. We know from the earliest historical records that the triune name Father, Son, and Spirit was lifted up during baptism. In 1873 an important document was found called the *Didache* or *The Teaching of the Twelve Apostles*. While the original date of the writing of the *Didache* is debated, it is widely recognized as the earliest Christian guide to discipleship. Chapter 7 of the *Didache* provides instructions on how to baptize people who have become Christians:

> *Baptize into the name of the Father, and of the Son, and of the Holy Ghost in living (running) water. But if thou has not living water, baptize into other water; and if thou canst not in cold, then in warm. But if thou hast neither, pour water upon the head thrice, into the name of the Father, Son, and Holy Ghost.[5]*

The early church debated whether a person should be baptized by immersion or by sprinkling, and not surprisingly, we still hear lingering discussions today on the proper way to baptize someone. The early church declared both forms of baptism equally valid forms of the sacred introduction into the Christian community. The single immersion, which is practiced in most evangelical churches today, represents God's unity. Triune immersion symbolizes God as a Trinity.[6] The practice of evoking the tri-une name of God at baptism has continued to be the common practice of Roman Catholic, Eastern Orthodox, and most Protestant churches.

The doctrine of the Trinity also found its way into the major creeds of the church such as the Nicene Creed. Originally adopted into the life of the Church in 325 AD, it was modified and expanded at the Council of Constantinople in 381 AD. [7] The updated Nicene-Constantinople Creed (also referred to as "the Nicene Creed") has been the guiding rule of faith for the Church for centuries. Nearly all Protestant Christians agree on the contents of the creed, and describe them as the essentials of the Christian faith. The word "Trinity" does not appear in the Nicene Creed, but the essence of Trinitarian faith is clearly seen. The creed opens with "I believe in one God..." and as Luke Timothy Johnson notes, "the Trinitarian character of the Christian God will progressively be unfolded by the creed, as it speaks in turn of the Son and the Holy Spirit."[8] The creed guides the confessor to acknowledge the Father as God, Jesus Christ as "Light from Light, True God from True God," and the Holy Spirit "who together with the Father and Son is worshiped and glorified."

Why is all this historical talk so important? I almost cringe whenever I hear that question. Perhaps you have been thinking the same thing. *Who cares what people 1,700 years ago thought about Jesus?* This thought may be more common among 21st century Christians than any of us would care to admit. I think a large number of Christians think the historic church has nothing to say to the modern church, but they would never admit it publicly. What a misconception of the Christian life people must have if they think the saints from ancient times have nothing to contribute to the present-day Church!

The Church is a community. It exists in local communities dotted all around the world. It also exists in a global community. If God is our Father and Jesus our older brother, then we are all brothers and sisters in God's family regardless of denominational affiliation, geographical location, or ethnicity. We will all worship together at the throne of God at the creation of the new heavens and earth, because God is ransoming people "from every tribe and language and people and nation" (Revelation 5:9).

The Church also includes a great "cloud of witnesses" and they surround us (Hebrews 12:1). They have fought many battles to pave the way for us. They labored to preserve the Scriptures and translate them into local dialects. Without the time, prayers, energy and effort of those historic saints who have gone before us, we would have no Bible, no form of worship, no gospel, and no faith. We not only honor their memory, but we can connect with them, sit at their feet and learn from them, through their writings.

Listening to the voices of the historical church may be too much *tradition* for young, hip evangelicals who are trying to build churches bigger and faster through slick marketing and hot-off-the-press organizational methodology. However, as Chesterton noted, "Tradition means giving votes to the most obscure of all classes, our ancestors."[9] Connecting with the writings of the historical figures like Ignatius of Antioch, Origin, Augustine, Thomas á Kempis, John Calvin, John Wesley, and Charles Spurgeon have added depth and strength to my faith. These men, among countless others, worshipped, preached, and confessed the Trinity centuries before I ever breathed a breath. I join them in their confession of faith in the triune God.

THE DOCTRINE OF THE TRINITY HOLDS TOGETHER ALL WE BELIEVE

All other Christian doctrines are held together by this one doctrine—the Trinity. Scripture is certainly the text of Christian faith and worship, but the doctrine of the Trinity is the orderly grammar that holds it all together.[10] James Torrance connects Trinitarian grammar with Christian worship. He writes, "The Christian doctrine of the Trinity is the grammar of this participatory understanding of worship and prayer."[11]

If you are completely honest you will admit that you are not a big fan of grammar. I am certainly not. I did not like grammar in elementary school. I still have awful memories of diagramming sentences in the fourth grade. I did not like grammar in high school when we had to write term papers. I did not like grammar in college, even though I was an English/ Writing major. I did not like grammar in seminary, and I do not like grammar now. There is nothing fun about grammar, but it is necessary. It is absolutely necessary if we are to use language to communicate in a meaningful way.

Language is not simply made up of words. The words we use in communication are little containers of the ideas that we are trying to convey.

True meaning cannot be communicated without some kind of overarching system to put our words together in a meaningful way. We need words and an agreed-upon system of rules to put those words together in order to effectively communicate. For example, I could say, *"All a supports have do loving in I wife who me I."* I am using all of the correct words, but I am not using them in a coherent, orderly way, and so the meaning of my message is lost. When I apply the rules of grammar and place my subject and predicate together and order my clauses correctly, then I can say, *"I have a loving wife who supports me in all I do."*

Message received. The rules of grammar are complicated and not always pleasurable to learn, but they are necessary. Grammar is taught, but more often it is passed on implicitly in any given culture. We have to teach the rules to correct common errors, but most rules of grammar are invisible. They are built into the way we communicate. Theological grammar is one of the primary functions of the doctrine of the Trinity.

The Bible uses words like God, Lord, Father, Son, Spirit, and one. "Trinity," while not in the Scripture, is the grammar that puts the biblical words together in a meaningful way. I have found when I view any concept discussed in the Bible through Trinitarian grammar then I stay balanced and centered. I remain historic and relevant at the same time. For example, the biblical doctrine of divine healing is best viewed through the Trinity. The Scripture reveals divine healing as proceeding from the heart of the Father through the ministry of Jesus by the Spirit's enabling power. By using the Trinity as a guide, we remain centered on God as our source for healing. The doctrine of the Trinity keeps us from ruts that say God no longer desires to heal today and from the rut that says healing is an automatic response to faithful (and faith-filled) prayer. These theological reasons explain in part why I am a Trinitarian Christian, and they lay the foundation for the more practical reasons.

STUDY GUIDE

1. What are some of the illustrations you have heard in an attempt to describe the Trinity?

2. Why do all human metaphors and illustrations fail to accurately describe God as three and one?

3. If the Trinity is such a crucial doctrine, then why isn't the word in the Scripture?

4. Have you ever been impacted by the writings of a historical Christian? How can you increase the influence of the historic Christians in your life?

5. How would the Christian faith change without the doctrine of the Trinity?

6. What topics in your faith tradition could be refreshed by viewing them through a Trinitarian lens?

Chapter Six

WHY I AM A TRINITARIAN CHRISTIAN: PRACTICAL REASONS

No sooner do I conceive of the one than I am illuminated by the splendor of the three; no sooner do I distinguish them than I am carried back to the one. When I think of any one of the three I think of him as the whole, and my eyes are filled, and the greater part of what I am thinking escapes me. I cannot grasp the greatness of that one so as to attribute a greater greatness to the rest. When I contemplate the three together, I see but one torch, and cannot divide or measure out the undivided light.

— GREGORY OF NAZIANZUS —

My pursuit of God has led me to this wonderful discovery of the Trinity. The Church did not create the doctrine of the Trinity, but discovered its reality through hundreds of years of prayers, sermons, worship, writing, and ecumenical councils. As I have been asked over the years why the doctrine of the Trinity is so central to my faith, I have come up with seven responses. In the previous chapter, I described the first three:

1. *The Bible reveals God as three-in-one.*

2. *The historical, orthodox, Christian Church confesses a triune God.*

3. *The doctrine of the Trinity holds together all we believe.*

The remaining four responses are of a more practical nature. They describe how the doctrine of the Trinity has shaped my identity as a follower of Jesus.

THE LOVE EXPRESSED IN THE TRINITY DRAWS ME INTO A COMMUNITY

We know God is love, and those who do not love do not know God; love is his essence (1 John 4:7-8). Biblical love is described with an outward focus. To love, as defined in the Scripture, requires other people. You can love your car, your cat, your dog, and even your goldfish, but that is not the biblical definition of love. We do not experience authentic love without other people. God not only loves others, he himself is love because for eternity there has been an ongoing love relationship between the Father, Son, and the Holy Spirit. These three persons of the one true God have been loving each other since before the creation of time. This triune relationship forms a holy community. There is no other being, no other relationship, no community in heaven or on the earth like our triune God.

God is a holy community, but he is also a community of love. His love causes him to look toward his creation. God the Father sends Jesus to be the doorway for those created in God's image to enter into the triune community. James Torrance describes Trinitarian community in terms of worship. He writes, "By his Spirit he (Jesus) draws men and women to participate both in his life of worship and communion with the Father and in his mission from the Father to the world."[1] The beauty and power of the incarnation and the death and resurrection of Jesus, places him in the position of mediator and usher into the eternal relationship between the Father and the Son.

I dislike the concept of the Father and the Son in an eternal relationship where the Holy Spirit is merely the bond of love between them. "The Spirit as the bond of love" is a popular Trinitarian description of the Holy Spirit. The idea goes back to Augustine who described God as the lover (the Father), the loved (the Son), and the love itself (the Holy Spirit). I see why some are drawn to this explanation of the Trinity.[2] It is Christ-centered and biblically verifiable. Nevertheless, I dislike any concept of the Trinity that depicts a relationship only between the Father and Son, because depersonalizes the Spirit who is "the Lord and Giver of Life." The Son has a special relationship with the Father, because he is the only begotten Son of God. Nevertheless the triune God has had an eternal relationship among all three persons. The Father, the Son, and the Holy Spirit have existed in a heavenly relationship for all eternity. And now God the Father, who is the head, opens up his two hands—the Son and the Holy Spirit. Through the Son's death and resurrection and the Spirit's outpouring, we have been invited to participate in this eternal relationship.

The triune God lived in self-existent harmony with himself. For all eternity, God has enjoyed the relationship he has experienced with himself, but because he is love, he opens up his infinitely happy community and invites us in. We were living our lives as strangers and orphans, isolated from our Creator. We were starving in spiritual poverty, completely separate from the eternal enjoyment shared among the Father, Son, and Holy Spirit. And then the Father sent his Son, and through his Son he sent his Spirit, to whisper in our ear, "*There is more. There is redemption. There is a kingdom. There is a unified community of holy love and you are invited in to celebrate and experience a relationship unlike any found on earth.*" As we turn by faith to the sound of his voice, we are whisked away into a soul-satisfying relationship with the triune God. We enter into the love and joy and warmth of family experienced in the center of the holy community of Father, Son, and Holy Spirit.

THE TRIUNE NATURE OF GOD UNDERSCORES THE VALUE OF RELATIONSHIPS

I recently repented before my congregation for an ongoing sin habit that I am ashamed to admit. For years, I have been dodging people at Wal-Mart. For our rural community, Wal-Mart has become the new city square. Everyone, it seems, goes to Wal-Mart—wealthy people, impoverished people, white people, Hispanic people, black people, and Asian people. When I set foot into Wal-Mart to get groceries, I am a man on a mission. I have my list of needed items. I mentally chart out my course so that I can make one sweeping loop through the grocery section without any wasted backtracking. I want to get in, quickly pick up my items, and get out. Speed and efficiency is the goal. If I stop to have a bland, ho-hum conversation with everyone I know, I will never escape, especially if I stop to talk to people in the church. So I devised a fail-safe plan. When I would see an unsuspecting church member on one side, I would quickly dart down the isle on the other side. What a fool proof plan! If executed with swift but careful attention, I could successfully avoid contact with everyone.

It was a good plan. It worked for years. I even made a joke out of it with some friends at church, but then Jesus had to detonate my plan with his whole *love your neighbor as yourself* requirement. As I wrestled with my cunning plan to avoid all human contact while shopping for groceries in light of Jesus' plan for me to love all these neighbors, I was struck with the value and priority Jesus places on relationships. Of all the things in creation, Jesus places high value on relationships. Darrell Johnson writes, "At the center of the universe is relationship,"[3] an eternal, mysterious, holy, loving relationship between the Father, the Son, and the Holy Spirit.

Jesus was once asked, "What is the most important commandment?" He replied without hesitation, "And you shall love the Lord your God with all your heart and with all your soul and with all your mind and with all your strength" (Mark 12:30). Jesus calls us not only to see the one true living God, but to give him all of our heart, love, energy, and attention. He concludes his response by adding a line from Leviticus 19:18, "The second is this: 'You shall love your neighbor as yourself.' There is no other commandment greater than these" (Mark 12:31). The second part to these dual commands of love is the command for us to give our heart, love, energy, and attention to other people. According to Jesus the greatest commands, upon which all other commands rest, are commands regarding the relationships we keep. Relationship with God and relationships with other people are most important, because God himself is an eternal relationship of persons.

THE MYSTERY DISPLAYED IN THE TRINITY DEMANDS MY WORSHIP

The Trinity as a primary doctrine of the church is a mystery, a sacred mystery. Bob Dylan poetically and prophetically captured the loss of mystery, the loss of sacred mysteries, with lines from his 1965 song, "It's Alright Ma' (I'm Only Bleeding)." Dylan writes that "disillusioned words" fly like bullets in a world where nothing is "really sacred."[4]

My entire spiritual journey has been in the context of an evangelical faith. I have rubbed shoulders with the writers, thinkers, preachers, and teachers who hold to the authority of Scripture, the exclusivity of Jesus, and the priority of the missional life of the church locally and globally. Certain movements and trends within contemporary evangelicalism have focused so pragmatically on evangelism that they have become orators of "disillusioned words," preaching a simplistic God, a God reduced to steps, methods, and principles, a God that can be used to enhance your life. Such disillusioned descriptions rob the central message of God and his gospel of its sacredness, its other worldliness, its mystery.

In stark contrast to this pragmatic, reduced God is the ancient doctrine of the Trinity, the proclamation of a God who is one, but not singular. Our God is a God who is mysteriously three-in-one, a God of one divine nature who has made himself known in three distinct persons, co-eternal and co-existing, a God without beginning or end. This God caused the psalmist to declare, "Great is the LORD, and greatly to be praised, and his greatness is unsearchable" (Psalm 145:3). His greatness is unsearchable, unverifiable, and without measure. It is a mystery we do not try to explain; it is a mystery we embrace. Steve Seamands writes,

> *In the presence of this mystery, we are no longer in a position of control where we can manage or master the subject. Before this Subject, worship is more appropriate than problem solving, awe is preferable to answers. So the mystery of the Trinity ought to evoke in us humility and worship—the very attitudes necessary for entering the circle of triune fellowship.*[5]

None of our earthly examples can explain the Trinity. All we can do is stand in awe and behold the greatness of his mystery.

I have been privileged to stand in front of two of the greatest mountain ranges in the world—the Colorado Rockies and the Himalayan foothills in North India. When you are standing in front of a massive mountain, there is very little you can do except stand there and feel small. You could take a ski lift up one and ski down. You could hike up the side of one to reach the summit. Both options bring with them an element of adventure, but for me, I stand in silence and gaze. There is something to the size and mystery of a mountain that evokes appreciation and awe. I have some geological concepts that help me understand how the mountain was created, but that does not change the wonder I feel standing in front of it.

The doctrine of the Trinity is not a logical riddle to try to solve; it is a mystery to be worshipped in awe and pure wonderment. People who get bored with God are people who do not reflect on the mystery of the Trinity. When we remove all the sacred mystery from God, we lose our passion in worship. I pastor a non-denominational church that prides itself in contemporary worship. If a song was written in the 1980s, it is too old. We want the latest, hottest worship song so we can be young, hip, and of course, contemporary. I enjoy singing a new worship song as much as the next guy. Yet if this feverous desire for the next greatest praise song is what drives our worship, we will quickly grow bored with the music and the God to whom we are singing. Reducing worship to technical elements and stylistic choices drains all the mystery out of worship. Quit worrying about the style of music and stand in awe and look. Take in the mystery. Embrace the mystery of the triune God.

THREE DOMINANT CHRISTIAN TRADITIONS CORRESPOND TO THE PERSONS OF THE TRINITY

My rediscovery and refueled pursuit of the doctrine of the Trinity has helped shape my identity as a Christian. Darrell Johnson had a similar experience. He writes, "I am often asked to identify myself using one of the theological or ecclesiastical labels of our times."[6] I have been asked similar questions when meeting new people, particularly when I meet new pastors. I suspect they want to know if I am on their team. They want to pigeon-hole me into one group or another in order to know if I am friend or foe. Johnson continues, "Am I Evangelical? Conservative? Reformed? Charismatic? If I must identify myself, I prefer the label "Christo-centric Trinitarian."[7] As I have rediscovered God as the Trinity, I have begun to answer similarly, except I drop the "Christo-centric" part. *What kind of Christian are you?* I am a Trinitarian Christian.

When people ask if I am a "charismatic," I don't know how to respond. I have spent most of my spiritual life in the Pentecostal/charismatic tradition. I completed a seminary degree at the oldest charismatic seminary in the United States. I serve a church born out of the charismatic renewal. I embrace the present-day reality of the gifts of the Holy Spirit, even the miraculous gifts. I believe God still heals people today and, here is the ultimate giveaway, I regularly pray using the private prayer language of the Spirit. However, when people ask me if I am a "charismatic," I simply do not know how to reply.

My response depends upon what they mean by "charismatic." If by "charismatic" they mean *charismania*, the Pentecostal/charismatic subculture of Christians who have a particular anti-intellectual spirituality, a sense of superiority about their spiritual experience, their own distinct way of talking about the Christian life, their own television shows, their exclusive group of media-driven teachers who have a leg up on truth, and who value worship services that are emotional and end in some kind of ecstatic experience—then I would say "no." Typically when Christians talk about "charismatics" they are referring to *charismaniacs* trapped in a Pentecostal/charismatic subculture. For me the label "charismatic" is not sufficient.

As I began to reflect on my own spiritual journey over the last few years, I realized my primary influences were coming from sources outside of the charismatic movement. I was not angry with anyone. I did not storm out of the charismatic movement because I disapproved. I think God simply led me out of a Pentecostal/charismatic subculture. I am taking with me the gifts of the Spirit, the expectation of miracles, and an experiential approach to the Christian life, but the "charismatic" label no longer describes my spiritual life. I have not rejected any of the key tenets of charismatic theology and practice, but I have opened myself up to other traditions within the Christian faith, and they have profoundly shaped me. I now consider myself a Trinitarian Christian.

As I reflect on the primary thinkers and Christian leaders influencing me today, I can see the three most influential traditions aligning themselves with persons of the Trinity. The three most influential traditions in my spiritual walk have been the reformed tradition, the evangelical tradition, and the charismatic tradition.[8] These traditions overlap and interrelate, but they seem to align most strongly with each of the members of the Trinity. The reformed tradition most strongly relates to the Father.[9] Thinkers and teachers from the reformed tradition such as Bruce Ware and John Piper have shaped me with their emphasis on the sovereignty and glory of God. The evangelical tradition most strongly relates to the Son. Evangelical leaders such as Bill Hybels and Rick Warren have influenced me with their emphasis on the work of Christ and the central role of evangelism in the church. The charismatic tradition most naturally lines up with the Holy Spirit. Teachers and heroes of the faith like Jack Hayford and Oral Roberts have inserted into my theological DNA a passion for the work of the Holy Spirit and the experiential Christian life.

SPIRITUAL TRANSFORMATION AND THE TRINITY

We are not the agent of our change, and neither are we the purpose and focus of our change. Spiritual transformation is the work of the Holy Spirit in changing us. We have a part to play in this process, and certainly our inner life is the stage on which the Spirit goes to work, but spiritual transformation has much more to do with God than it does with us. God is the engineer, the agent, and the model of our transformation. It is his plan, his work, and his example. To use the language of the Trinity, *spiritual transformation can be described as the work of the Holy Spirit to transform us into the image of Jesus for the joy of God the Father in the context of Christian community as we walk along spiritual pathways.*[10] In other words spiritual transformation includes (1) the Spirit's work, (2) the Son's image, (3) the Father's joy, (4) Christian community, and (5) spiritual pathways.

Spiritual transformation can be viewed from a variety of vantage points, but a Trinitarian vision keeps transformation God-centered and worshipful. L.T. Jeyachandran also sees a connection between the doctrine of the Trinity and spiritual transformation. He writes, "Three self-giving, self-effacing persons constitute the amazing God whom we worship! It is this aspect of God's character that we seek to reflect in our life and walk as the church of Jesus Christ."[11] A Trinitarian vision protects us from the subtle temptations from the kingdom of self, the temptation to make spiritual transformation just another individual, privatized self-help program. If any one of the five components of this Trinitarian vision is missing, an unhealthy preoccupation with self is the inevitable outcome.

Without the Spirit's work, people move towards a legalistic form of the Christian life. Without focusing on the work of the Spirit to transform us, people typically fill the void with willpower. Transformation is no longer a willingness to open up to the Spirit's power and work, but it becomes an individually produced program solidified by rules, regulations, and religious practices that are measurable and controllable. This form of discipleship and sanctification is no longer a spiritual journey, but a humanly-created religious program. This attempt at transformation without the

Spirit's work can only be transferred by a system of rewards and punishments. When the Spirit works to transform the human heart, the human participants are freed from the duty of transforming themselves. We are no longer in control of our spiritual development. We become authentic shape shifters as we rely on the Spirit's power to transform us.

Without the Son's image, people move towards a subjective form of the Christian life. Christ is the central figure of discipleship, and without his presence in spiritual formation, people do not have a standard by which to gauge their spiritual growth or transformation. With no immovable standard, they move inward to define what they will be transformed into according to their own subjective interpretation of the Scripture. Furthermore, the element of worship is lost because Christ would not be present to behold, and thus we would not know what kind of person we were becoming. With Christ present, spiritual transformation has a common vantage point within the community of faith. We are each becoming unique expressions of the image of Jesus.

Without the Father's joy, people move toward a consumer form of the Christian life. The Father's joy provides the ultimate purpose of spiritual transformation. The Father receives joy when people are conformed into the image of Jesus because transformation is the Father's predestined plan for us.[12] Furthermore, the Father is overjoyed as people are transformed into the image of Jesus because the Father loves the Son. He loves the Son with an eternal love, a love that caused him to declare from heaven, "This is my Son, whom I love; with him I am well pleased" (Matt. 3:17). If people do not pursue spiritual transformation in order to please the Father's heart, the temptation is overwhelming to make spiritual transformation a means for self-improvement. People would then view transformation as a way to make themselves better so they would be more useful to the Christian community or society. With the pursuit of the Father's joy, spiritual transformation takes on an eternal purpose. People become shape shifters not for themselves or for their benefit but for the sheer purpose of pleasing the heart of God the Father.

Without Trinitarian community, people would move towards a privatized form of the Christian life. They would assume they are able to become transformed by themselves without connecting with other Christians in the local church. The loss of Trinitarian community removes the context of transformation. With Trinitarian community, spiritual transformation takes on the corporate identity of the local church and opens up the individual heart to the Spirit's work through other people.

Without spiritual pathways, Christians can become lazy, forgetting their responsibilities. Those who are being transformed do assume a passive position, but allowing the Spirit to do the work of transformation does not imply that the human participant has nothing to do in the process. As Christians we can walk along certain pathways in order to partner with the Holy Spirit. To refuse to walk down any pathway would hinder his work. The spiritual pathways that foster the work of the Spirit are the classic spiritual disciplines, well trodden paths that have been walked by Christians for centuries. Before we begin our walk on the spiritual pathways, we have to look up and catch a glimpse of the Father's joy.

Chapter Seven

THE FATHER'S JOY

Jehovah, the living God, is described as brooding over his church with pleasure. He looks upon souls redeemed by the blood of his dear Son, quickened by his Holy Spirit, and his heart is glad. Even the infinite heart of God is filled with an extraordinary joy at the sight of his chosen.

— CHARLES SPURGEON —

One of the joys of being a dad is watching my children grow and change. It is difficult to see the change right before my eyes. In order to gain some perspective, I have to look back at pictures of when my boys were a few years younger to see how they have changed. My wife is an avid scrapbooker. She has albums upon albums filled with pictures of our boys framed with creative cut-outs, stickers, and journal entries describing the event surrounding the pictures. Recently, we had some missionaries from India in our home, and my wife pulled out the scrapbooks to show them what our boys looked like when they were younger. I watched from a distance as she opened up the books. Questions and comments turned into smiles and laughter as the missionaries flipped through the pages. I joined the men around our dining room table and began to tell the stories that went along with the pictures. I had forgotten some of those memories. I could not believe how much my boys have grown.

My oldest son Wesley has certainly changed over the years. When he was younger he struggled to control his emotions, particularly when he lost a game of some kind—an unfortunate trait he inherited from his father. I cannot deny my competitive tendencies. When I was a child, I particularly hated losing. I used to avoid playing sports where I could not be competitive. *If I could not win, why play?* I can remember being in a bowling league when I was ten or eleven and being the weakest player on our four-man team. Often a series of gutter balls would leave me in tears. Wesley has the same trait to a heightened degree. He has teared up and attempted to run away from the game more than once whether it is soccer, baseball, card games, or board games.

One of the first years he was playing soccer, the coach put him in at goalie. He is tall and pretty fast, but he lacked practice time in the goal. I coached him from behind the goal with my very limited soccer knowledge. In one game, the other team made a break for Wesley's goal. One of their faster kids broke away from the herd and sped his way towards the goal. The kid had some skills. He made one move and sent Wesley defending the wrong side of the goal. He kicked the ball with the force of a World Cup athlete and...*Goal*! Embarrassed and dejected, Wesley turned his back to the field and looked at me with a mixed look of anger and disgust. Large tears began to well up in his eyes as the referee set the team up for a kick off. I bent down and encouraged him. I reminded him that he had a job to do. His team was depending on him. I told him, "It's okay to feel sad and even to shed a tear or two, but you cannot allow your emotions to keep you from doing your job. You have to protect the goal."

He composed himself and turned to face the field. After some time, the same World Cup athlete broke out from the herd with the ball. I could see Wesley's feet begin to shift back and forth quickly. He was preparing himself with his knees bent and hands outstretched. It is funny how time seems to go into slow motion in moments like that one. It seemed to take forever for this speedster to move the ball down the field. As he took a shot at Wesley's goal, I held my breath. Wesley moved over into position and in an instant, he caught the ball. *No goal*. Wesley made a great save.

He slung the ball back into play and turned around with a huge grin. I clapped my hands and gave him a thumbs-up signal. I too broke out into a smile. I was overjoyed not because he made a great save, but because he controlled his emotions and continued to play his part on the team even after he had been beaten. He was changing. Today as I see him working to control his emotions and make good choices, I realize he is still changing. He is growing up and changing into a man after God's own heart. He still has a way to go, but I can see progress. I can see change, and it brings me unspeakable joy.

God the Father also takes joy as his children change. As the Holy Spirit shapes us into the image of Jesus, God the Father receives unspeakable joy. The pleasure and joy that God the Father experiences is the ultimate purpose for our spiritual transformation. We become shape shifters ultimately for the Father's joy. Certainly, we receive significant benefit from being transformed. We are better people the more we reflect the image of Jesus, but our benefit is not God's definitive purpose in changing us. He transforms us for his own joy.

It is difficult for twenty-first century evangelical Christians living in North America to understand that the Father's joy—and not our own personal benefit—is the ultimate purpose of spiritual transformation. We are in a consumer-driven culture where everything seems to be bought and sold in order to make our individual privatized lives better. Whatever we need for a more fulfilling life can be purchased, normally at the low, low price of $19.95. New cars, movie tickets, music downloads, books, health equipment, and even prescription drugs can be purchased at a reasonable cost to improve our lives and make us more satisfied, more complete human beings. So we buy it, drive it, watch it, read it, use it, and pop it, but still the elusive satisfied life continues to escape us.

We have even tried to market the gospel of Jesus to meet the felt needs of consumers. I have fallen into that trap. There is nothing wrong with marketing and advertising events, programs, activities, and ministries within the local church, but when our marketing feeds the consumerism of Christians and non-Christians connected to our local churches, they get the wrong message. They wrongly assume God exists merely to meet their needs. The God of the Bible becomes reduced to the image of Santa Claus, the jolly old elf who drops into our lives to fill our stockings with goodies. Consumer-driven Christians wrongly assume that the Christian faith can be boiled down to a handful of basic principles to help them have a better life. Unfortunately, our methodology is inextricably tied to our message. How we communicate the truth of the spiritual transformation says something about transformation itself and the God of transformation.

While God does desire to transform us for our own good, his deepest desire is to transform us for his own joy. Our eyes need to be fixed on this great end: we are shape shifters for our Father's continual joy. He is, after all, the happy God, the joyful God. He made known to us the mystery of his plan through Jesus because it brought him joy.[1] Jesus revealed the truth of God not to the wise and learned, but to simple little children for the joy of his Father.[2] God experiences a full range of emotions including the jubilation of joy.

THE HAPPY GOD

It is difficult to separate the emotion of happiness from the virtue of joy. I have heard some people try to make a case for true spiritual joy without happiness. Once I heard a pastor describe how extra time in prayer had brought him a greater amount of joy, and yet he said this with the most emotionless, staid, and sober expression on his face. Draining all the happiness out of joy causes joy to lose its earthy vibrancy. Granted, happiness can ebb and flow in intensity, but there is nothing less noble about its expression in the human life. Joy as discussed in the Scripture is inextricably tied to happiness—not a silly, giddy, childish kind of happiness, but a deep and abiding sense of satisfaction.

"Happy" is a fairly good synonym for the biblical word "blessed." There cannot be a more over-used and misunderstood word in contemporary evangelical Christianity than this word "blessed." It has reached number one on the list of *Greatest Words in Christianese*. Have you ever heard a conversation before a worship service when a pious-looking man is asked, "How are you today, Bob?" *I am blessed. I'm blessed. The family is blessed. We're blessed! God bless you.* I have challenged Christian people over the years to try to pray without using the words "bless," "blessed," or "blessing." *Father God we thank you Father God for your blessings Father God and we just ask that you bless Aunt Suzie Father God with your blessings and we praise you Father God that we are blessed Father God in Jesus' Name.* I am not implying that we should not use the word. I am only arguing that we should know what it means.

"Blessed" as used throughout the Bible has a variety of meanings depending on how it is used, but "happy" is a common connotation for the word. In Paul's first letter to Timothy, he uses the word "blessed" in reference to God. He discusses sound doctrine "that conforms to the glorious gospel of the blessed God" (1 Timothy 1:11). The word "blessed" can be used to mean "favored by God." In this appearance of the word, such a meaning would not make much sense. God is favored by himself? This reference is a place where "blessed" means "happy." God is the happy God.[3] The gospel of the death, burial, and resurrection of Jesus is the message of the happy God. We have to be careful not to reduce God to being only the happy God. God is simultaneous the holy God, the good God, the wrathful God, the sovereign God, and the gracious God. Nevertheless, we cannot allow the picture of the wrathful God to overshadow the picture of the happy God. He is a God of joy, a God of eternal happiness.

THE HAPPY GOD OR THE HAPPY ME

We have been given the wonderful invitation to share in God's joy. Jesus made it clear; his teaching and his commands were a way for us to share in his joy and for our joy to be made complete.[4] The question is not so much whether we ever experience joy. The question is whose happiness are we living for? Are we living lives in pursuit of our own happiness or the happiness of another? Do we work and strive to make our own happiness full and complete or do we focus our energy on the happiness of others? In God's kingdom we can only gain what we lose. We can only get what we give away. If we live in pursuit of our own happiness, then true joy eludes us. If we give up on the pursuit of happiness for ourselves and live for the joy of God the Father, then we get to share in God's joy. In the end we will see both a happy God and happiness for ourselves, but we begin with the pursuit of the happy God.

Such a life spent in bringing God happiness is completely counter-intuitive to us. We live in a culture shaped by the pursuit of personal happiness. One of the founding documents in the formation of the United States of America expresses the pursuit of happiness as an "unalienable right" given to us by Nature's God, our Creator. If we are told that "Nature's God" has given us this right, then it naturally follows for the pursuit of happiness to become a cultural assumption. Jesus, who represents not "Nature's God" but the living God, the maker of heaven and earth, proclaimed a kingdom of God's reign and rule, where God's people would live not for their own happiness, but for the happiness of God. The tension between this kingdom value of the preeminence of God's happiness and the cultural value of the preeminence of individual happiness presents great difficulty for Western evangelical Christians. *When was the last time you ever did anything purely for the happiness of anybody you know, let alone God?*

When my wife and I were first married, my Dad made it a point to ask us about grandchildren nearly every time we were together. It became a running joke in our family. We knew when the family was getting together there would be the question, "So when can we expect a baby?" My Dad really wanted to be a Paw-Paw. One Christmas we wanted to play a joke on him. We wrapped up a jar of baby food to give to him as a Christmas present. My wife was not pregnant, but we knew he would assume she was when he opened his jar of baby food. My parents were living in California at the time, and we flew out to be with them at Christmas. As we gathered around the living room to exchange gifts, my eyes were glued on Dad as he handled the wrapped jar of baby food. He focused on the wrapped jar with an inquisitive look. When he unwrapped the jar and saw the baby food label, he looked up, eyes wide open with that you-are-about-ready-to-make-a-baby-announcement look. I smiled and said, "Dad, we have bought this jar of baby food for you to feed to your grandchild. Notice the expiration date is five years down the road. Maybe you will have the opportunity to feed your grandchild *one day*. We are not pregnant!" The room broke out in laughter.

When my wife did become pregnant we did want to do something to surprise my parents with the big announcement. We had a custom ball cap made up for my dad with the phrase, "I am going to be a Paw-Paw." It was Christmas time, as fate would have it, and so we wrapped up the hat to give to him as a Christmas present. It seemed fitting to make the announcement around the same holiday when we had pulled our previous prank. My parents had come out to our apartment near Christmas time, and we had set up a time to exchange gifts. We held the wrapped hat until the end of the gift exchange, and with my heart pounding nearly out of my chest, I gave him the wrapped box. As he opened the box to reveal the hat, he studied the words carefully. He looked up again at us, but this time with an I-am-not-falling-for-this-again look. He said, "Yeah, I am going to be a Paw-Paw, *someday*." With a big grin, I replied, "No, you are going to be a Paw-Paw soon. Jenni is pregnant!" My mom said, "No, you are not having a baby." I said, "Yes." My Mom and Dad said, "No." I ran to the bedroom and got the stack of pregnancy books Jenni had been reading, and I slammed them down on the coffee table and said, "We are having a baby!" My Dad's face exploded with joy. We hugged and cried. He was happy.

As followers of Jesus we are living for the joy of our heavenly Father. The Holy Spirit is working to change us into the image of Jesus for the joy of God the Father. In a culture dripping with self-service, self-indulgence, and individual happiness, Jesus is calling us to be subversive, to live for the happiness of Another, to make God the Father's joy the ultimate intention of our life. We are being transformed for his joy, the joy of the happy God.

GOD THE FATHER'S JOY IN GOD THE SON

God receives the most joy from himself. At first this seems like an incredibly ego-centric statement. If anyone standing on the earth would make a similar statement, we would be quick to correct them. And yet God's happiness and pleasure is most perfectly and rightly found in himself. Jonathan Edwards opens "An Unpublished Essay on the Trinity" with these words:

> *It is common when speaking of the Divine happiness to say that God is infinitely happy in the enjoyment of Himself, in perfectly beholding and infinitely loving, and rejoicing in, His own essence and perfection, and accordingly it must be supposed that God perpetually and eternally has a most perfect idea of Himself, as it were an exact image and representation of Himself ever before Him and in actual view, and from hence arises a most pure and perfect act or energy in the Godhead, which is the Divine love, complacence and joy.[5]*

God is the only one who can rightly find happiness within himself. The difference between God's enjoyment of Himself and a professional athlete declaring, "I love me *some me*," is God's communal nature. A person is a single entity, and God exists as an eternal community. For a human being to declare self-love as the highest source of joy violates biblical descriptions of love, but God can love himself and find exceeding joy in himself, because he is a self-giving community of Father, Son, and Holy Spirit.

God's infinite enjoyment with himself is clearly seen in the relationship between God the Father and God the Son. Jesus referred to God as his Father. He even called God, *Abba* in Aramaic, which would sound something like "Daddy" in contemporary English. In the earthly relationship between God the Father and Jesus the Son, we see a glimpse of the eternal relationship between these two. God is able to find complete joy with himself because in Trinitarian community the Father undoubtedly loves the Son. Joy overflows where love abounds. And while Jesus walked the earth, he made it clear—the Father loves the Son.

Many of his fellow Jews were unable to tolerate Jesus' seemingly blasphemous habit of calling God his Father. When some of the Jewish leaders exploded with anger over Jesus' audacity to heal someone on the Sabbath, Jesus replied that he was simply doing his Father's work. Jesus explained with humble conviction how his teaching, and authority, and ministry of healing were all imitations of what he saw his Father doing. *Why would God show Jesus, a simply tradesman from the backwoods of Nazareth, his heavenly work?* Jesus gave a simple response, "for the Father loves the Son." [6]

Jesus was, and is, loved by his Father in a much deeper and intimate way than any purely human relationship. The Father loved the Son because Jesus willingly gave his life as a sacrifice. Jesus' life was not taken from him as he was arrested, falsely accused, tried, beaten, mocked, and ultimately executed. He courageously and thoughtfully laid down his life, with the promise "only to take it up again" (John 10:17). The Father watched his Son's bravery, and he loved him. The Father never turned his back on his Son, during Jesus' passion and ultimate death. Under intense agony and rejection, Jesus cried out, "My God, my God, why have you forsaken me?" Jesus felt abandoned, but the Father never forsook his Son. He loved the Son and honored him for his great sacrifice.

The Father's love for the Son was not only dependent upon what the Son did, but who the Son was. The Father felt great love and joy for Jesus and declared it openly, even before Jesus began his public ministry. Jesus met John the Baptist at the river to be baptized. As Jesus came up out of the waters of baptism, the Holy Spirit descended on him in the form of a dove, and God the Father spoke from heaven in a beautiful picture of Trinitarian life. The Father's words were not a private exhortation to the Son, but a public declaration of his love and joy for his Son. In a booming and bellowing voice he declared, "This is my Son, whom I love; with him I am well pleased" (Matthew 3:17). *Is there a more powerful statement in the life of a son?* The Father's joy in his Son began before Jesus ever taught large crowds of people along the seashore, before he cured the lame and the sick, before he fed thousands, and before he restored dignity to the oppressed.

The joy the Father found in the Son was not conditional. He loved his Son before Jesus began his ministry, and yet the Father's love was deeper than even Jesus' humble incarnation. As Jesus prepares for his pending arrest at the end of his life, he prays for his followers, "*Father, I want those you have given me to be with me where I am, and to see my glory, the glory you have given me because you loved me before the creation of the world*" (John 17:24). The Father's love for the Son is an eternal love.

GOD'S GLORY IN GOD'S JOY

Why not the glory of God? Why would God's joy, and not his glory, be the ultimate goal of spiritual transformation? There is no denying the importance of pursuing God's glory. The Westminster Shorter Catechism, used by Presbyterians and other churches with a Reformed background, teaches basic Christian doctrine. It opens with the question, "What is the chief end of man?" The answer is simple—*Man's chief end is to glorify God, and to enjoy him forever*.[7] Human existence and purpose is rightly defined in terms of God's glory. We do exist to glorify him, to live with him for his glory and our enjoyment of him certainly brings him glory. John Piper has coined the phrase "Christian hedonism" to describe how our joy is connected to God's glory. Piper's often quoted phrase, "God is most glorified in us when we are most satisfied in Him," expresses the connection between God's glory and God's joy.[8] God is glorified as we enjoy him, and God is glorified in himself as he enjoys himself. God's glory rests fully in his joy, the joy he finds in himself and the joy he sees in the image of his Son.

STUDY GUIDE

1. What have you purchased in the last ten years thinking it would bring you true satisfaction, but it did not?

2. When was the last time you went out of your way to make your father, or some other father figure in your life, happy?

3. Have you used the word "blessed" and not really known what it means? How does your definition of "blessed" compare with the definition of happiness?

4. When people are happy, they laugh. What do you think makes God laugh? List three examples from the past week of incidents that may have caused God to laugh.

5. What is most powerful about God the Father declaring his love for Jesus even before Jesus began his public ministry?

6. How is God's glory connected to God's joy?

Chapter Eight

THE SON'S IMAGE

"He who follows Me, walks not in darkness," says the Lord. These are the words of Christ by which we are told that we should imitate His life and manners if we want to be truly enlightened and delivered from all blindness of heart. Let our chief endeavor, therefore, be to meditate upon the life of Jesus Christ.

— THOMAS Á KEMPIS —

No single individual in human history stands out more than Jesus Christ. It is good and right to call the Son of God by this name, but "Christ" is more of a title than a name. His name is Jesus. When the angel appeared to Joseph to explain why his wife-to-be was pregnant, he told Joseph to name the child "Jesus," because the child would "save his people from their sins" (Matthew 1:21). Names were extremely important in Jewish culture, and the name "Jesus" meant something like "God is our salvation" or "God rescues us." While it is appropriate to call Jesus by the title "Christ," it is not his name. It is not even his last name. If Jesus was given an assigned seat at school they would not put him in the front of the class after Miss Adams and the Mr. Barkley. "Christ" is a title meaning "anointed one," referring to the Jewish practice of pouring oil over the head of a new king. The Jews referred to this anointed one as Messiah. In the twenty-first century, we would translate it "King." Christ Jesus is King Jesus. "Christ" is his kingly title, but Jesus is his name and the name "Jesus" is used twice as often as "Christ" in the New Testament.[1] There is something powerful about his name.

WHAT KIND OF JESUS

Jesus is downright popular these days. He continues to show up in surprising ways in popular American culture. From the "Jesus is my homeboy" craze of a few years ago to the frequent cameos Jesus makes on television shows, there is no denying Jesus' popularity is at an all-time high. He shows up on *The Simpsons, The Family Guy, South Park, Saturday Night Live* sketches, and in stand-up comedy bits. Mel Gibson made a graphically violent movie about the torturous death of Jesus, and everybody went to see it. Since 2004, *The Passion of the Christ* has grossed more than $370 million.[2] Jesus has popped up in songs by Kanye West, Carrie Underwood, and Kid Rock. His name even made it to the cover of Kid Rock's 2007 album, *Rock N Roll Jesus*—although I take it on good authority that Kid Rock is not singing about the same Jesus sung to by millions of Christians around the world.

In April 2008, *American Idol*, one of the most popular shows on American television, closed their "Idol Gives Back" charity episode with the contestants forming a choir to sing, "Shout to the Lord." Most notable in the performance was the absence of the name "Jesus." The opening line "my *Jesus*, my Savior" was changed to "my *shepherd*, my Savior." The next episode, which aired the very next day on April 10, 2008, opened with the contestants singing "Shout to the Lord," but this time they sang, "my Jesus, my Savior." Jesus seems to be popping up everywhere in pop culture. In 1966, John Lennon said the Beatles were more popular than Jesus, but now four decades later, I think we can say that Jesus is more popular than the Beatles.

Newsweek ran a cover story in March 2005 entitled "How Jesus became Christ." The story included a poll related to a typical American's thoughts regarding tenets of the Christian faith. The poll revealed:

- *78 % of Americans believe Jesus rose from the dead*

- *75% say he was sent to the earth to absolve mankind of its sins*

- *81% say they are Christians[3]*

There is no denying the popularity of Jesus in popular American culture, but I want to know what kind of Jesus 81% of Americans claim to follow. If eight out of ten Americans call themselves Christians, then which Christ, which Jesus, are they following? Is it the Mormon Jesus? This Jesus was a pre-existent human spirit who was born as a man and achieved the status of godhood. Is it the Jehovah's Witness Jesus? Their Jesus is another god separate from God the Father, who never resurrected from the dead. Is it the Muslim Jesus ("Isa" in Arabic)? This Jesus was a prophet, but was somewhat lacking in full revelation of the nature and will of God. *Is it the self-help Jesus? The Jesus of popular American humanism? Is it the good moral teacher Jesus? Is it the "help me when I am in trouble" Jesus? Is it the prosperity Jesus? Is it the soft, weak, effeminate Jesus? Is it the "God just wants me to happy" Jesus? Which Jesus is it?*

If we are to proclaim Jesus as the Savior to rescue us from our sin and become the image of our transformation, then we absolutely must be right on who Jesus is. We might disagree on church government, on the gifts of the Spirit in the life of the local church, and on the inter-relatedness of predestination and free will. In our churches we may disagree on the style of music used in public worship, the color of the carpet, and on various means of Christian education, but we must agree on Jesus. We must rightly understand who Jesus is.

GETTING JESUS RIGHT

In case you have forgotten, the entire life and ministry of the local church is about Jesus. We worship Jesus, serve Jesus, pray to Jesus, teach Jesus, preach Jesus, and give all we have to Jesus. The local church is the visible body of Jesus. We are his hands extending love and compassion to those who are in need. We are his feet walking to serve others. We are his mouth proclaiming the truth of his kingdom. We are the living stones of the Church that Jesus is building. Within us and among us, Jesus receives the first place, the place of preeminence. Our very existence as Christians is by Jesus, through Jesus, and for Jesus. It is easy for a local church to become fixated on so many different tangential, secondary, mundane issues and forget this truth—to be a Christian is to be rescued by Jesus (through his death, burial, and resurrection), to follow Jesus (through prayer, worship, study, reflection, and other disciplines), and to be transformed into the image of Jesus (by the work of the Holy Spirit). It is, in reality, all about Jesus.

One could argue that the triune God is the focus of the Church. One potential pitfall in giving so much attention to Jesus is forgetting about God the Father and particularly God the Holy Spirit. Some Christian traditions have overlooked the Holy Spirit, because they give so much attention to Jesus.

Nevertheless, it seems appropriate to be both Christ-centered and Trinitarian in scope in the ministry of the local church. It is certainly right to be Christ-centered in our approach to the Christian life. God is Father, Son, and Holy Spirit, but within the Trinity there is a "revelatory bulge" with the Son. God has chosen to reveal himself most vividly through God the Son, who is Jesus. At one point in his earthly ministry, Jesus so boldly declared, "Anyone who has seen me has seen the Father" (John 14:9). God the Father chose his only Son to represent him and God the Holy Spirit works to draw attention back to the Son. Jesus himself said that when the Holy Spirit comes he would, "bring glory to me by taking from what is mine and making it known to you" (John 16:14). God has revealed himself most clearly through Jesus.

Disciples of Jesus today are standing in a tradition of nearly two millennia of Christians, who have worshiped the triune God in the context of Christ-centered life. Jesus receives the focus and attention, even though during his lifetime, Jesus did not do the things that normally bring people such global attention. He never wrote a book. He never earned an academic degree. He never held a political office. He never led an army into battle. He never started a business and made a lot of money. He never owned property. He never married. He never had children, but this one simple, solitary life sparked a revolution that has continued for two thousand years. He may be one of the most recognizable figures in Western civilization, and he is the kind of person we shape shifters are becoming.

JESUS OUR HUMAN EXAMPLE

Jesus is the pattern of our transformation. In his letter to the churches in Galatia, Paul writes, "My dear children, for whom I am again in the pains of childbirth until Christ is formed in you..." (Galatians 4:19). The Holy Spirit is working to change us on the inside to look like Jesus. If we are going to be conformed into the image of Jesus, we need to carefully reflect on the Jesus of Scripture, on the Jesus of historic, orthodox Christian faith. While there is not enough room here to explain all we believe about Jesus, perhaps most foundational is this phrase: Jesus is truly God and truly man. The Nicene Creed declares,

> *We believe in one Lord, Jesus Christ, the only Son of God, eternally begotten of the Father, God from God, Light from Light, true God from true God, begotten, not made, of one Being with the Father.*[4]

Jesus, who lived as a real human being, is true God, from true God. While we worship Jesus as God, we are being transformed into the image of his humanity, not his divinity.

This is in direct contradiction to the Jesus of the Church of Jesus Christ of Latter Day Saints. The Mormon Jesus is not the one, true living God, but a separate god who is an example of what people can become. Brigham Young University's Frequently Asked Questions about the Church of Jesus Christ of Latter-day Saints provides the following question and answer regarding their doctrine of godhood.

Question: What is the Latter-day Saint understanding of godhood?

Answer: All of God's children have within them a divine nature with the potential to become like him. To become more like God, individuals must gain increased light and truth and follow all the commandments that God has given.[5]

The Mormon Jesus is not the only begotten Son of God, but the first of many spirit children of God. If you follow the commandments of Jesus, then you can become a god just like Jesus. We who follow the Jesus of the orthodox, Christian faith are being changed into the image of Jesus as truly man, not as truly God.

JESUS OUR PERFECT EXAMPLE

The Holy Spirit is in the process of reshaping us to look like Jesus in his humanity. Sin has made us ugly, devoid of life, and subhuman. Jesus is the example of someone fully human and fully alive, someone truly free from sin. He is the pattern for perfect humanity, the example of what a human being should look like. He "made himself nothing, taking the very nature of a servant, being made in human likeness" (Philippians 2:5-7). He never stopped being God, but he "made himself nothing," literally he emptied himself of his power and authority as God, so he could live as a real human being.

Jesus is our example, but he first saves us from our sin before the Holy Spirit can change us into his image. Spiritual transformation does not put us in a place where God will accept us. God accepts us by grace through Jesus' death, burial, and resurrection. Transformation does not put us on the road towards God in our spiritual journey. Jesus puts us on the road through the cross and the empty tomb. We can only expect to be transformed into the image of Jesus after God has rescued us and we have made Jesus the boss of our life.

Jesus is the perfect example of being fully human, because he never sinned although he was tempted. Jesus lived in a real physical body. He lived and worked in a real first-century Jewish family where he faced all the temptations and pressures of any ordinary man. Jesus' true humanity and real temptation is wonderfully illustrated in Anne Rice's *Christ the Lord: Road to Cana*, a fictitious account of the life of Jesus around the time of his baptism and miracle at the wedding of Cana. Rice masterfully portrays the inner struggle of Jesus as he wrestles with the calling of his heavenly Father versus his very human desire for marriage.[6] Jesus was tempted in every way we are, "yet was without sin" (Hebrews 4:15).

From a life of purity and holiness, Jesus is our example of how to live a fully human life of obedience in perfect relationship with God and other people. He is the pattern of perfect humanity. He is our example of moral character. He is the model for ethical behavior. Such a pure and holy example would be overwhelming if transformation were fueled only by human willpower. N.T. Wright adds that reflecting on the life of Jesus can make us depressed. He writes,

> *Some people's lives really have been changed simply by contemplating and imitating the example of Jesus. But observing Jesus's example could equally well simply make a person depressed. Watching Richter play the piano or Tiger Woods hit a golf ball doesn't inspire me to go out and copy them. It makes me realize that I can't come close and never will.*[7]

If spiritual transformation was a matter of copying the life of Jesus, I would be utterly depressed. However, shape-shifting into the image of Jesus is possible, not by human effort, but by the transformative work of the Holy Spirit.

The Holy Spirit works like a master sculpture with one eye on Jesus and one eye on our hearts, as he takes hammer and chisel to our inner life. Michelangelo was once asked how he sculpted his masterpiece, David. He replied that he simply chiseled away everything that did not look like David.[8] The Holy Spirit is at work to transform us into the image of Jesus by chipping away everything that does not look like Jesus in our life. Specifically, the Spirit is changing us to (1) think like Jesus by giving us his mind, (2) feel like Jesus by giving us his heart, (3) love like Jesus by giving us his attitude, (4) ultimately act like Jesus by empowering us with his actions.

THE MIND OF JESUS

In sculpting us to reflect the image of Jesus, the Holy Spirit is changing us to think like Jesus. The mind of Jesus is a mysterious thing. We know that he "grew in wisdom and stature" (Luke 2:52). A part of Jesus empting himself was laying aside his omniscience. He did not know everything, but as any human child he had to learn and grow intellectually. The mind of Jesus presents itself with a number of questions. As an adult, what did he know? How much did he know about himself? How aware was he of his divinity and his incarnation? How much did he know about creation? Such speculation does not bring answers, but adds to the intrigue.

Jesus' mind is a mystery, and in a mysterious way we have the mind of Christ.[9] Jesus did know the God he loved. He had an intimate relationship with God his Father, and so he had an intimate knowledge of God. Jesus had a mind shaped by the Scriptures. As a child Jesus was found in the temple courts listening and questioning the elders, and everyone who listened to Jesus was "amazed at his understanding and his answers" (Luke 2:47). He devoted himself to the study of Scripture, and whether he was tempted by the devil or suffering on the cross, he could recite words from the sacred text. The Holy Spirit is at work shaping our minds to reflect the mind of Jesus, so we think like Jesus, and view other people like Jesus, and process things like Jesus.

THE HEART OF JESUS

Jesus was filled with a certain kind of passion, a certain kind of affection. His heart was fully submitted to the will of his Father. On one occasion, the disciples asked Jesus to eat something. He oddly responded that he had food they knew nothing about. They were concerned about his physical needs; Jesus was concerned about their spiritual needs. Jesus explained, "My food is to do the will of him who sent me and to finish his work" (John 4:34). It was the desire of his heart to do what God the Father wanted. Jesus had given his heart to the will of his Father.

Dallas Willard has developed a model of spiritual transformation using the acronym VIM—vision, intent, and means.[10] A person who experiences transformation needs an adequate vision of their transformation. *What will they look like when they are transformed? What does a fully transformed person look like?* In Willard's model, Jesus is the vision of our transformation. From this point, most people look right over the intent and go right to the means, the pragmatic "how to" in the process of spiritual transformation. The centerpiece of Willard's VIM model is "intent." There must be a "want to" in addition to the "how to." A person must have the desire to be transformed in order to participate with the Spirit's work. The Holy Spirit himself shapes our affections, giving us the desires of Jesus, the heart of Jesus, so that we desire the things Jesus desires.

THE ATTITUDE OF JESUS

Closely related to the heart of Jesus is the attitude of Jesus. We are reminded as Christians that our attitudes should be the same as that of King Jesus.[11] Attitudes are those deep-seated motivations that influence our actions. Jesus' attitude, his primary motivation, was love. The love Jesus displayed was not a sappy, sentimental, cheap, greeting card kind of love. Tina Turner asked in 1984, "What's love got to do, got to do with it? What's love but a second-hand emotion?" A "second-hand emotion" does not describe the love that motivated the heart of Jesus. His love was a go-the-extra-mile, turn-the-other-cheek kind of love. His love was a touch-the-untouchable, heal-the-incurable, love-the-unlovable kind of love. It was the kind of love that took him to the cross.

Jesus emphatically explained this kind of love with the most shocking statement: *love your enemies*. Everybody loves the people who love them. The love pulsating through the heart of Jesus was a love even for his enemies. At the cross, while Jesus was enduring unthinkable, excruciating pain, he prayed for his Father to forgive those who were killing him. As the Spirit works to change us to reflect the image of Jesus, he gives us this kind of love. He pours this kind of love out into our hearts.[12] This work of the Holy Spirit is one of the most unique aspects of the Christian faith. Every major world religion has commands, rules, or precepts, but the uniqueness of Christianity is the commands with the promise of transformation and power to fulfill those commands. The Holy Spirit gives us God's love by shaping our attitude to be one of love, just like Jesus.

THE ACTIONS OF JESUS

All of the Spirit's work in transformation is ultimately designed to bring outer change, to change the way we live. Jesus demonstrated his love by acts of compassion. He told his disciples, "My command is this: Love each other as I have loved you. Greater love has no one than this, that he lay down his life for his friends" (John 15:12-13). He demonstrated his love by the way he lived. He made the ultimate demonstration of love by becoming our substitute, taking our sin and the wrath of God, for us. He refused to allow his love to remain internal; it shaped the course of his life.

The Spirit is changing us to ultimately act like Jesus. To claim that we are shape shifters who ultimately act like Jesus does not mean we will become clones. The more we are being transformed to look and act like Jesus, the more unique we become. Some of us will choose to welcome back John Mark, some of us will not.[13] Some of us will choose to eat meat sacrificed to idols, and some of us will not. Some of us will choose to drink alcohol in moderation, some of us will not. Some of us will listen to popular music, some of us will not. Some of us will choose to home school our children, some of us will not. The beauty in the Holy Spirit's work in changing us to reflect the action of Jesus is the diversity. As we are all being changed to act like Jesus, the Holy Spirit will lead us in different ways, always in love, but in ways that are increasingly unique.

STUDY GUIDE

1. Why do you think Jesus is so popular these days?

2. Is it easier for you to think of Jesus as divine or as human? Why?

3. What do you think temptation for Jesus was really like?

4. In what areas of your thinking or thought life do you need the Holy Spirit to give you the mind of Jesus?

5. When do you seem to lack the heart of Jesus?

6. With whom in your life do you have the hardest time maintaining a Jesus-like attitude of love?

7. What one thing in your life least resembles the life of Jesus? What do you need to do to change that area of your life?

Chapter Nine

THE SPIRIT'S WORK

Our great need today is a new openness, a new readiness to approach the Holy Spirit, a reawakened longing for the Spirit. Now that we have knowledge enough to explore the immense horizons of cosmic space in one direction and subatomic particles in the other direction, only the Holy Spirit can give human kind that sustenance of soul, that love which will prevent our humanity from shriveling up altogether as a result of our own knowledge. Only the Holy Spirit's help will make us able to use our technical knowledge not to destroy but to humanize our planet and improve the lot in life of every person.

— RANIERO CANTALAMESSA —

The Holy Spirit is God's agent upon the earth.[1] All the work God the Father has ordained to carry out through the death, burial, and resurrection of Jesus, he does by the Holy Spirit. Spiritual transformation, as a part of God's redemptive plan to make us more human, more like Jesus, can never be accomplished by direct human effort. Dallas Willard describes spiritual transformation as a "Spirit-driven process."[2] The Holy Spirit is the spiritual component in our journey of *spiritual* transformation. In my shape-shifting journey, I have continually asked, "So what is the Holy Spirit doing to change me to look like Jesus?"[3] I deeply desire to open myself to his work and partner with the Holy Spirit. I have given up on self-help methodologies, whether Christian or secular. Personal will-power has failed. I am relying solely on the Spirit's work to change me to look more like Jesus. My actions are only a response to his work in order that I may participate with the Spirit. As I have searched, studied, prayed, and reflected, I have uncovered more than a few activities of the Holy Spirit in the process of spiritual transformation. These activities are overlapping and inter-related, but they are listed individually, so we can better understand the Spirit's work and cooperate with him.

BECOMING BY BEHOLDING

Seeing verses in different Bible translations gives us an opportunity to look at an individual verse in a slightly different light. One of the key spiritual transformation verses is 2 Corinthians 3:18. The *New King James Version* renders it, "*But we all, with unveiled face, beholding as in a mirror the glory of the Lord, are being transformed into the same image from glory to glory, just as by the Spirit of the Lord.*" We do not use the word "beholding" in everyday speech. While the NIV uses the phrase "reflect the Lord's glory," it is the KJV and the NKJV that use the phrase "beholding as in a mirror." In Greek, the phrase is all one word, and it refers to looking in a mirror. The word in the context of the verse should read: "*We who have unveiled faces are the ones who are looking at ourselves in a mirror and we are being transformed into his likeness with increasing glory by the Spirit*" (author's translation).

Beholding our image in a mirror takes time. It is not a passing glance or a casual look. The verse has two ideas that are fused together—"the ones looking in a mirror" and "being transformed by the Spirit." The Spirit is transforming us by causing us to behold Jesus. My youngest son Taylor is mildly autistic. When he was younger he would avoid eye contact, and sometimes I would gently grab his chin and direct his face to my face and say, "Look at Daddy." The Spirit does a similar work. He grabs our spiritual faces and redirects our attention to Jesus so we can gaze upon Jesus—who is the mirror. We will become like Jesus as we keep our eyes focused on him.

FUELING DESIRE

Any talk of "desire" among Christians typically carries with it a negative connotation. Desire has led people to do some foolish things in the name of Jesus, but desire in and of itself is not the problem—the strength of desire is not really even the problem in the Christian life. The problem with desire is not its strength, but its object. When we desire things outside of

God's plan, desire can become twisted. The issue with twisted desires is not that they are strong, but that they are misdirected. C.S. Lewis writes,

> *Indeed, if we consider the unblushing promises of reward and the staggering nature of the rewards promised in the Gospels, it would seem Our Lord finds our desires not too strong, but too weak. We are half-hearted creatures, fooling about with drink and sex and ambition when infinite joy is offered us, like an ignorant child who wants to go on making mud pies in a slum because he cannot imagine what is meant by the offer of a holiday at the sea. We are far too easily pleased.*[4]

Temporary desires do not compare to the desire for God, which is much stronger. A passionate person is not lead astray by the strength of his or her passion, but by the object. Romans 12:11 exhorts us to "keep (our) spiritual fervor...." The phrase "spiritual fervor" means desire born of the Holy Spirit. There are certain Christian traditions that do not emphasize desire. Some Christian traditions elevate a stoic rationalism over spiritual desire. The extinguishing of desire is not Christian at all; it is much closer to a Buddhist worldview. The Holy Spirit does not want to erase all our desires. He wants to redirect our desires in a righteous direction. The Holy Spirit wants to redirect our desire:

- *From self service to a desire to serve others*

- *From obsession with material things to worship in the presence of the Father, Son, and Holy Spirit*

- *From self-centered love to a desire for relationship with God*

- *From a lust for power to a desperate dependence upon God, our strength*

- *From a need for recognition to a holy passion for His fame*

- *From a need for acceptance to a desire for biblical community*

- *From anger and frustration to developing a heart of a warrior, ready to battle the enemies of the soul*

- *From selfish pleasure to a holy hunger for the kingdom of God and the joy unspeakable that is found there*

THE POWER GENERATOR

Energy drinks have become popular over the last few years. I am not much of a fan, but I can understand why people are looking for the next thing that will give them the energy to do more in less time. We are all looking for more energy to get things done. Anything in motion needs fuel to keep going. Work, owning a home, school, friends, family, media, hobbies, and even the local church can drain us of energy. The stress of life can turn our productivity into lethargy. We need energy. Fortunately, for us who are Christ followers, there is a "pick me up" that is caffeine-free, sugar-free, and ephedrine-free. It is all natural and abundant in supply. This *it* is a *he*. The Holy Spirit is at work within us "energizing and creating in you the power and desire" to become Christ-like.[5]

The power we can create on our own is commendable, but it is never enough. To express a Jesus kind of love requires that we be a certain kind of person—a person who has been recreated in the image of Jesus. And this act of becoming requires a Jesus kind of power—a power generated by the Holy Spirit. The Christian life is not a matter of willpower, but a willingness to open up to the Spirit's power. Willpower will always cause us to crash, just like the energy crash from a high-sugar diet. We have to quit trying to be a Christian in our own power and open up and allow God's power to shape us to look like Jesus by the power of the Holy Spirit.

A MORAL COMPASS

Jesus promised that the Holy Spirit would come to guide us into all truth.[6] "He will guide you" reinforces the journey metaphor when describing the Christian life. Our life in the kingdom of God has experiences, but it is a journey. It is easy to chart our growth as Christians in momentary experiences. "God saved me on *this* date." "I was baptized on *this* day." "I had a powerful encounter with the Holy Spirit on *this* day." "God called me to lead a Bible study on *this* date." These watershed moments are good and important, but they make up about .5% of your entire Christian life. 99.5% of your Christian life is spent in ordinary moments. We need the guidance of the Holy Spirit in the mundane, everydayness of life.

We need a guide when we do not know where to go. On my first trip to India, I had an overnight stay in Amsterdam on the way home. I was staying at the Youth With A Mission (YWAM) base on the harbor in the downtown, touristy area of Amsterdam. I decided to go and find something to eat, so I headed out into the city. One of the YWAM staff members asked me if I wanted a map. I said "no" and kept walking. This moment was when I made my mistake.

I started down the street along the harbor. I was determined to stay on the road along the water so that I could easily find my way back. I was walking along the harbor for about 45 minutes looking for a place to eat. I thought I might find a local pub and try some Dutch food when out of the corner of my eye, I caught the most beautiful sight that I have ever seen. Up one of the streets, I saw a red sign shining bright that beacon of American values—I saw, in all of its shining glory, the yellow glow of the golden arches. After eating rice and curry for three weeks, I was starving for a quarter pounder with cheese and a large order of fries. I darted up the street, departing from my plan, and went into the McDonald's. I ordered. I sat. I ate. I licked the salty goodness off my fingers. I was happy.

I left McDonalds and saw a flow of people going into the downtown area. I could have chosen to go back towards the harbor, but I let curiosity get the best of me, and I went into town, my second mistake. After walking around for about an hour, I decided to head back to the YWAM base. "The harbor should be just the next street over," I thought. Wrong. I wandered around for about 30 minutes, when I realized I was lost. I had no map and more importantly, I had no guide. I debated about walking about 4 kilometers to the bus station, because there were signs to the bus station. In the end, I decided to grab a taxi. The taxi driver spoke just enough English. After a brief conversation, he understood where I wanted to go. I hopped in the taxi. He made a left and then a right, and there we were in front of the YWAM base. The whole ride took about 45 seconds. I was so embarrassed. I was less than a block from the base the whole time. The entire embarrassment of a 45-second ride could have been avoided if I had a guide. In our Christian journey the Holy Spirit is the guide. He leads us through this journey of life. He is our constant companion, ready to guide us through the uncertainties of life. He shapes our will by pointing us towards the will of God. He makes us wise by pointing us in the right direction.

WRITING ON OUR HEARTS

The immutability of God is a theological constant. "I the LORD do not change" (Malachi 3:6). He is faithful, reliable, and trustworthy. Thomas Chisholm penned the words:

Great is Thy faithfulness, O God my Father;
There is no shadow of turning with Thee;
Thou changest not, Thy compassions, they fail not;
As Thou hast been, Thou forever will be.

God does not change. There is not even a hint of turning in him. God does not change who he is. He is no shape shifter, but he does change how he deals with his creation. His actions in history have changed based on covenants. If we are going to understand how God is changing us, an understanding of covenant is essential.

In ancient times, covenant was a contractual agreement initiated in blood between two parties. It was a pledge of lifetime loyalty, provision, and protection. God's story begins with the covenant he made with one man, Abraham, who became the father of a nation—Israel. The Old Testament is a record of God's agreement with Israel, but the New Testament is God's agreement with the entire world, both Jews and non-Jews. In the Old Covenant, God's law was almost all external, written down in moral codes. In the New Covenant, God's law is mostly internal, written on our hearts by the Holy Spirit. The New Covenant does contain written laws, but God's primary way to lead us through this new law is by his Spirit.

The Holy Spirit shapes our conscience by writing God's law in our hearts. He takes the written commands, such as "love God with all of your heart, mind, soul, and strength," and "love your neighbor as yourself" and changes our conscience to process moral decisions by the law of God. A law written on our hearts does not give us license to do whatever we *feel* is morally right. The Holy Spirit also works through the Scripture and the accountability of the local church to guide us. We still need to hear the voice of the Spirit through Scripture and the local church, but we no longer need external legalistic rules concerning what we should and should not do.

SLAYING THE GIANT WITHIN

A person cannot overly sanitize the Christian life. It is difficult, hard, painful, and uncomfortable. The Scripture describes the Christian life with metaphors like "die to your self," "I am crucified," "crucified the flesh," and "circumcision of the heart." Christians in the early church debated whether to circumcise Gentile Christians according to Jewish customs. In the end, the Church agreed not to require circumcision, because salvation was by grace through faith alone. The circumcision required of all followers of Jesus is a circumcision of the heart, a cutting off of the kingdom of self.

Self is a malevolent monster, a giant who desires to rule our hearts. When the kingdom of God clashes with the kingdom of self, there can only be one winner. The kingdom of God comes with a sword to slay self. Just as Jesus was raised from the dead, so our self can be raised to life in a new form. The Spirit does not work to change us by obliterating the self, but by dethroning it through a death, burial, and resurrection of the self. The new self, the resurrected-from-the-dead self is infused with a new identity. The new self is empowered by the Spirit with humility and a new desire for righteousness and holiness.

Speaking a New Name

Kids can be mean. Listen to how they talk to each other on the playground, when they think there are no adults listening. Not all kids are mean, but on every crowded playground you can find kids who use their words as missiles, and they fire their weapon at will. No weapon is more popular than name-calling.

As I was growing up, I seemed to be picked on constantly by other kids. Maybe I am just hyper-sensitive to it, but I felt like I never measured up to my peers and was always being picked on and called names as a child. I remember one occasion when I was a freshman in high school. I had endured the long hours and early morning practices and made the basketball team. I was awkward, clumsy and my desire for the sport far outweighed my talent, but I survived the final cuts. At one practice, we were all headed to the water table to get something to drink during a break. There was a bag of ice on the table next to the cups and pitcher of water. I reached into the bag and quickly tried to grab a handful of ice cubes. When I pulled my hand out, I sent ice flying out of the bag and sliding across the gym floor. *Oops.* I then heard one of my teammates yell in my direction, "Vreeland, you _____." I will let your imagination fill in the blank, but I can promise you it was not a word of encouragement. As we grew up, I became friends with that guy, but I never forgot the name he called me. It stung. It stuck with me. It felt like a heavy rock that had been chained to my neck.

I think name-calling hurts because words are powerful. Proverbs 18:21 is true. "The tongue has the power of life and death…" We teach children that words will never hurt us, but the reality is words can pack a powerful punch. Hurtful names carry with them the power of death. Even untrue names can create the sick feeling of death inside us. A name does not have to be true in order to hurt. Often hurtful names like "worthless" and "stupid" stick with us and form an ungodly identity. One of the most powerful changes in our lives occurs when God the Holy Spirit speaks a new name in us. We cannot become shape shifters with hurtful names weighing us down.

Isaiah rightly prophesied the day when God would call us by a new name: "The nations will see your righteousness, and all kings your glory; you will be called by a new name that the mouth of the LORD will bestow" (Isaiah 62:2).

The Holy Spirit calls us by a new name, giving us a brand-new identity. These names are filled with the power of life. These names change the view we have of ourselves and put to rest the old, hurtful names. We become transformed by the Spirit as we are called by new names like: *loved*, *accepted*, *righteous*, *chosen*, and *elected*.[7]

The overwhelming temptation when experiencing the Spirit changing our identities is to assume he gives us new names to make us feel better about ourselves. God the Holy Spirit changes our name from "worthless" to "loved" and from "rejected" to "accepted" because of what God the Son accomplished for us for the joy of God the Father. We do receive a boost in self-esteem, but self-actualization is hardly the point. It is freeing to understand our new identity in Christ. It is freeing to hear the Holy Spirit speak a new name in our hearts, but the Bible warns us: "Do not use your freedom to indulge the sinful nature; rather, serve one another in love" (Galatians 5:13). The Spirit changes our identity by giving us a new name to make us fully human, so we can serve and love others.

CHANGING MY MIND

Renewing our minds is an integral part of the Spirit's work in transformation. The Holy Spirit uses the Scripture as a sharp instrument to shape our minds so we can think like Jesus. Our thinking is connected to our decision-making and our emotions. When making a moral decision, we typically process things in our minds, weighing the pros and cons and determining which action is right. Having determined the right thing to do, we act. Our thinking is also interrelated with our emotional life. Our emotions are affected by a number of factors such as diet, exercise, stress-management, and hormones. Nevertheless, our thought life plays a critical role in how we experience our emotional life. For example, people's emotional reaction to seeing a dead cat on the side of the road is determined by what they think about cats. If people are indifferent when it comes to cats, then when they pass by a dead cat on the side of the road, they will drive on with no emotional reaction. If they are cat lovers, then they may be moved to tears. And if they drive by *their* beloved cat, then they would be emotionally devastated. Our thinking affects a variety of components of our human life.

Renewing our minds is not so much what we do, but how we partner with the Holy Spirit. Our minds are renewed by the Scripture, which requires us to open up the Book from time to time. As we read the Scripture the Spirit guides us into all truth by shaping our minds to think God's thoughts. There are certain brands of popular American Christianity which cause us to think too shallowly about God and too deeply about ourselves, *our* needs, *our* wants, and *our* entertainment. The Spirit re-conditions our minds to think less about our wants and needs and more about the beauty and mystery of the triune God.

BECOMING MORE HUMAN

Sin is a problem. Sin is *the* problem. It is the problem not only because of its psychological and sociological effects, but for its effects on the human heart. Sin is the reason why we need to be transformed by the Holy Spirit. Sin is both our act of willful disobedience to a known law of God (John Wesley's definition), but it is also a deep rooted corruption of our human nature. Sin has a way of making us into something devoid of life, something ugly, something less than human. As we confess our acts of willful disobedience, God forgives us, but we still need the work of the Holy Spirit to reverse the effects of sin in order to make us more human, more like Jesus.

David understood the depth of sin's distortion of our true humanity. Five times David asks to be cleaned, cleansed, or washed in Psalm 51. He makes his passionate plea known to the Lord. He cries, "Create in me a pure heart, O God, and renew a steadfast spirit within me" (Psalm 51:10).

The stain of sin is an awful enemy to fight. It keeps our true humanity hidden. As the Holy Spirit cleans us of the stain of sin, our true selves begin to emerge. He creates, or recreates, in us a new heart, a new human spirit cleaned from the stain of sin. This process allows us to become shape shifters, transformed into the people God intended us to be, very unique expressions of Jesus.

The Holy Spirit begins to remove the stain of sin by conviction. Jesus said,

> But I tell you the truth: It is for your good that I am going away. Unless I go away, the Counselor will not come to you; but if I go, I will send him to you. When he comes, he will convict the world of guilt in regard to sin and righteousness and judgment: in regard to sin, because men do not believe in me; in regard to righteousness, because I am going to the Father, where you can see me no longer; and in regard to judgment, because the prince of this world now stands condemned. (John 16:7-11)

Conviction is not the same as condemnation, the lingering voice of our old self attempting to hold us back by sins of the past. Condemnation makes us less human. Conviction is the activity of the Spirit in identifying sin and its stain. He convicts us of three things: (1) *sin*, the self's way of thinking and acting; (2) *righteousness*, God's way of thinking and acting; and (3) *judgment*, the consequences or rewards of choosing one over the other. Conviction can be deeply painful, but its purpose is always to change us and bring our true self to the surface.

GODLY DISPLAYS OF AFFECTION

Why do so many Caucasian Christians have trouble displaying affection for God? Affection is not emotionalism, and it is not a secondary characteristic in our love for God. A purely rational, stoic approach to the Christian life is not God's design. A passionate heart is central to the Christian faith. Jonathan Edwards writes, "True religion, in great part, consists in the affections."[8] Affection is our desire; it is related to our "want to." The Holy Spirit will come to us and poke us and prod us, but he does not want us to come to God under compulsion. He wants our "want to" to catch up to our "ought to."

The Holy Spirit stirs up our affection and ignites it with a passion for God. Unfortunately, Christians who have once experienced the Spirit transforming them from dead, lifeless religion to true godly affection often turn to outside excitements in order to regenerate those feelings of passion. They turn to high-energy, emotionally-charged worship services or so-called "revival" meetings packed with large crowds and some kind of sensational religious side-show to ignite their affections. God the Holy Spirit does not need outside entertainment to stir our affections. Some of the most transformative moments of godly affection for me have been quiet moments of worship, reflection, or study.

HEALING MY FEELING

One of the most powerful transformative works of the Holy Spirit is healing damaged emotions. Personal pain and tragedy have a way of warping our interior lives. We cannot expect to become more like Jesus if we are carrying around hurts from the past. Unforgiveness, depression, bitterness, abuse, exploitation, grief, and similar experiences can weight heavy on our hearts, preventing the image of Jesus from being seen. To be fully transformed into the image of Jesus, we need true emotional health. Peter Scazzero links emotional health to spiritual health. He rightly pointed out that many Christians neglect their emotional hurts. He writes, "The problem is that when we neglect our most intense emotions, we are false to ourselves and close off an open door through which to know God" and become transformed by God the Holy Spirit.[9]

The Holy Spirit changes us by healing our damaged emotions in surprising ways. Often he works through long-term recovery with the help of a Christian counselor and support group. Sometimes the Holy Spirit breaks through in momentary experiences of healing, when people are set free from emotional bondage. I have a pastor friend who described an experience of emotional healing whereby he was left completely transformed. He had struggled with feelings of rejection for a long time. Even after preaching he would seek out affirmation, due to these overwhelming feelings of rejection. He always compared himself to his brother, and he never felt like he measured up. Many of the feelings of rejection were rooted in a long-term romantic relationship that ended while he was in college. After the relationship ended, he was suicidal. By the grace of God, his life was spared, and God called him into the ministry.

He married and started a family while he served as a youth pastor. His life and ministry were all progressing with fruitfulness, but he continued to suffer from overwhelming feelings of rejection. During a worship service at their church, a guest minister was preaching on unforgiveness. At the end of the service, my friend sensed the presence of the Holy Spirit. He lay on the floor in the church and began to cry. He stayed there for nearly two and a half hours feeling the Holy Spirit sweep over him in powerful waves of healing. He stood after that experience completely transformed by the Holy Spirit, transformed by a powerful encounter with the healing work of the Spirit.

STUDY GUIDE

1. How would you describe your relationship with the Holy Spirit?

2. Why do we become like Jesus by focusing on him? Is it possible to live a life beholding Jesus and never be transformed into his image?

3. What do you do when your desire for the kingdom of God is distracted by a desire for something else?

4. How do you respond in those seasons of life when you do not feel so passionate about Jesus and your spiritual life has run out of fuel?

5. When has the Spirit directed you in an unexpected way?

6. Which laws do you need the Holy Spirit to write on your heart today?

7. How has your identity been changed by new names given to you by the Holy Spirit?

8. Has there ever been a time when the Spirit has healed you from an emotional wound? Describe your process of healing.

Chapter Ten

CHRISTIAN COMMUNITY

And we always keep together; and for all things wherewith
we are supplied, we bless the Maker of all through His Son
Jesus Christ, and through the Holy Spirit. And on the day
called Sunday, all who live in cities or in the country gather
together to one place, and the memoirs of the apostles
or the writings of the prophets are read, as long as time
permits; then, when the reader has ceased, the president
verbally instructs, and exhorts to the imitation of these
good things.

— JUSTIN MARTYR —

The doctrine of the Trinity is the gift of the historic church to the modern church. In our desire to make our local churches contemporary, it is easy to forget the wonderful gifts given to us by the early church. Since the time when Jesus instructed his disciples to baptize in the name of the Father, Son, and Holy Spirit, the early followers of Jesus wrestled with the nature of God. Jesus called God his Father. He himself professed to be the Son of God and he discussed the Spirit of Truth, the Helper, the Holy Spirit who would come after he had left. The discovery made by the early church was that God the Father, Jesus, and the Holy Spirit were together the one true God. They did not create the doctrine of the Trinity as much as they discovered it through countless years of study and reflection. There is no more important revelation concerning the nature of God than what the early church revealed. God is a Trinity, one God, one divine substance, revealed in the three persons—Father, Son, and the Holy Spirit.

Community in God's Tri-unity

When we speak of the Trinity, our attention quickly goes towards the distinctness of the persons and not the mystery of the unity God. If you were to ask the average Christian sitting in an average evangelical church on Sunday morning to describe the doctrine of the Trinity, the average Christian would probably describe the Trinity as the Father, Son, and Holy Spirit. The distinctness of the persons commonly stands out in our reflection of the Trinity, and such a tendency can cause us to miss the unified oneness of the Trinity. It is like we cannot see the proverbial forest for the trees. These three persons—the Father, Son, and Holy Spirit—exist in a single, unified, holy community.

We are allowing the doctrine of the Trinity to guide us in understanding spiritual transformation. The Holy Spirit is changing us to look like Jesus, and this process does bring joy to the heart of God the Father. Yet this Trinitarian vision does not end with the distinct persons, but continues with the unified community. *God, who is a holy community, is changing us in the context of a holy community, the local church.* When Paul mentored Timothy in the ministry of the local church, he shared his concern with how people relate to one another in what he calls, "God's household, which is the church of the living God, the pillar and foundation of the truth" (1 Timothy 3:15). Those of us who are followers of Jesus are his body here on earth. We are God's family. As God's household the local church is also the pillar and foundation of God's truth. From the platform of the local church God has chosen to communicate his truth through the proclamation of the gospel and the teaching of Scripture. And God has chosen the local church to be the canvas on which the Holy Spirit repaints the human heart to reflect the character of Christ.

The Local Church and the Universal Church

The local church is the context in which God demonstrates his truth by transforming us into the image of Jesus by the Holy Spirit for his own joy. We can learn things about Jesus apart from the local church, but we cannot authentically and fully become like Jesus if we distance ourselves from the Church. There are those who claim to be a member of *God's* Church even though they are not a member of *man's* church. For them, participation in a local church is unnecessary. Their lack of connection with the local church is based, in part, on a faulty view of the Church in the Scripture.

The New Testament has two ways of talking about the church. In some places the Bible is referring to the local church and in other places it is referring to the universal Church. The Greek word for "church" is *ekklesia*. It is roughly translated "gathering." When reviewing biblical references to "the church," we have to decide if the text is describing the local gathering and a universal gathering.

Since the Reformation, Protestant Christians have identified certain characteristics that distinguish the local church from the universal Church. The local church is:

1. *Visible*

2. *Indefinite in number*

3. *Diverse in style and belief systems*

4. *Composed of only living people*

5. *Led by recognized, biblically-qualified leaders*

The local church is first of all *visible*. You can see it. The local church is not a building of wood or brick and mortar. It is composed of living stones, people who have been called by God. The local church is also *indefinite in number*. There are literally hundreds of thousands of local churches around the world meeting in steeple-topped buildings, renovated store-fronts, warehouses, homes, movie theaters, elementary schools, and in secret locations around the world. These local churches have a *variety of styles and belief systems*. We believe the same things regarding essential matters like the nature of the triune God and salvation. These essentials are reflected in the historic creeds of the Church.[1] On the essentials of the faith we are in agreement. We differ in non-essential areas like musical styles, worship traditions, modes of baptism, church government, and the expression of the gifts of the Holy Spirit. These local churches are composed of *living people* and they are governed by *recognized, biblically-qualified leaders*.[2]

In contrast to the local church is the universal Church,[3] the universal gathering of followers of Jesus. The universal Church is:

1. *Invisible*

2. *One*

3. *Consistent in core doctrines*

4. *Composed of living people and dead people*

5. *Led by Jesus*

The universal Church is *invisible*. Although it contains living people, the borders of this Church cannot be seen. There is only one Church.[4] The gathering Jesus began building with his original twelve disciples has continued to the present day. We are all a part of this Church, and we confess the same essential *core doctrines*. This Church includes *living people and dead people*, and *Jesus is the leader*. He is the chief shepherd, the senior pastor of the universal Church.[5]

THE FOUNDATION OF THE LOCAL CHURCH

God, who is a holy community, is changing us shape shifters in the context of a holy community, the community of faith. The Holy Spirit works through the universal Church and the local church. We can all stay home and claim to be a part of the universal Church, but if we are not connected to a local church, we cannot call ourselves Christians. The local church is not a building of stone, wood, or steel. According to John Calvin, the local church is the gathering where "the word of God (is) purely preached and heard, and the sacraments administered according to Christ's institution."[6] The visible gathering of fellow Christians where the word of God is preached and the sacraments administered under recognized, biblical leadership is the context in which God demonstrates his truth by transforming us into the image of Jesus by the Holy Spirit for his own joy. We can know God without the local church, *but not intimately*. We can experience God without the local church, *but not fully*. We can learn about the faith without the local church, *but not completely*. We can begin to be transformed into the image of Jesus without the local church, *but only to a degree*.

TRANSFORMING THROUGH "ONE ANOTHERING"

The Holy Spirit changes us as we obey the "one another" commands. We are not the Spirit's transformation workshop simply because we show up for worship on Sunday morning. We become the context for spiritual transformation as we fulfill the numerous "one another" commands recorded in Scripture.[7] The New Testament contains nearly fifty commands calling us to do certain things for "one another." These commands are the reason why you cannot stay home, watch Christian television, tell all your friends what you think about organized religion, and call that "experience" church. You cannot fulfill the "one another" commands in individualistic, privatized religion. You cannot serve one another (Galatians 5:13) or be kind and compassionate to one another (Galatians 5:13) if you distance yourself from the local church. On the contrary, as we invest our lives in a local community of faith and begin to fulfill these commands, we give the Holy Spirit a foundation to do his transformative work. While each of the "one another" commands contributes to the life of the local church, five in particular are vital in the Spirit's transformative work—*submit to one another, pray for one another, teach one another, spur one another on towards love and good deeds*, and *love one another*.

SUBMIT TO ONE ANOTHER

Whenever I lead couples through premarital counseling and I address the subject of biblical roles for a husband and wife, I lead them to Ephesians 5. Before I discuss the husband's call to love his wife and the wife's command to submit to her husband, I draw their attention to the first preceding verse: "Submit to one another out of reverence for Christ" (Ephesians 5:21). Submission in marriage is in the greater context of mutual submission to each other out of our reverent submission to Christ. As Christians, we are called to submit to one another.

In the land of the free and the home of the brave, the call to submit can be a jagged little pill to swallow. The word *submission* carries with it a number of negative connotations. It conveys images of oppression and exploitation. However, biblical submission is the source of freedom. We experience true freedom only when we are submitted to King Jesus. Once we have submitted to him, Jesus calls us to submit to one another. A local congregation of shape shifters who are submitted to the purposes of God the Father, the lordship of Jesus, and leadership of the Holy Spirit becomes the place where the Spirit is free to change their hearts.

We do not automatically submit ourselves to fellow Christians the instant we go through the membership process of a local church. In order to submit to each other, we need to trust each other. We build trust by spending time with the people in our local church. Attendance in weekend worship services is vital, but getting to know the people in our local church requires small groups, dinner invitations, lunches together, and other social engagements. Trust develops over time as we begin to open up with one another. In order to trust each other, we need to be vulnerable. Superficial conversations designed to keep people out of our "personal lives" will do nothing to build the trust that real submission requires. In order to be open, we need to be broken people. Producing authentic brokenness is a process of honestly reflecting on our own weaknesses and frailty. If we portray ourselves as having our entire lives in order, we will never become open and trustworthy.

Brokenness is not a matter of self-loathing cynicism. Hating yourself will cause you to lose your soul. Brokenness is an honest awareness of your own struggles and an open heart towards the Spirit's shape-shifting work. A closed heart leads toward judgmentalism and hypocrisy, in which you judge others for their frailty and ignore your own weaknesses. People with a closed heart quickly condemn the sin they see in others and, just as quickly, hide their own sin. A broken heart openly and honestly confesses sin to God and develops a plan for repentance. Brokenness leads to openness; openness leads to trustworthiness; trustworthiness leads to real submission.

A contemporary word for submission is *accountability*. When you chose to submit yourself to a small group of people, you are asking them to hold you accountable to your plan of repentance. You are asking them to be an open door of confession, a living place where you can confess your sins to each other (James 5:16). As you seek to submit yourself to one another, consider the following suggestions.

1) *Be honest with the sin in your heart.* Stop justifying your sin. Stop rationalizing it, and stop ignoring it. Do not over-sanitize your soul with the repetitive confession, "I am the righteousness of God in Christ." Deal honestly and ruthlessly with the sin still living in your heart. You will never seek to submit to others if you continue ignoring the junk in your heart.

2) *Confide in the people in your church whom you know and respect.* Invest in relationships with leaders in your church and others who are mature in the faith. Once you have built a friendship with one or more people you have grown to trust, confide in them.[8] Confess your sin to them. You need to confess your sin to God. However, confessing your sin to other people opens the door for the Spirit to work through a human relationship to cleanse and change you.

3) *Develop a plan to live differently.* Authentic, biblical repentance includes determining how you will live differently as a result of your confession. Ask the people who receive your confession to help you come up with a plan to live differently. Construct a plan that is reasonable. Within the plan, develop a set of contingency plans, just in case the first plan falls through. Include a list of "what will I do if..." statements. Think through as many pitfalls as possible.

4) *Ask them to check in on you.* Once you have developed a plan of repentance, ask those holding you accountable to stay in touch with you. Confession and repentance in the confines of a mutually submitted group of fellow Christians is a powerful experience. The difficulty comes the day after you and your accountability group develop a plan of repentance and you start working the plan.

5) *Submit to them when they call you back to your plan of repentance.* Do not get angry when you drift from your plan and your accountability group attempts to call you back to the plan. Give them permission ahead of time to call you back to repentance any time you begin to deviate, and then do not become frustrated with their pleas. Give them permission to call you names the moment you begin to drift. The name "slacker" is one of my personal favorites when I, or my friends, begin to backslide.

PRAY FOR ONE ANOTHER

The prayers from your lips can become powerful tools in the hands of the Holy Spirit. You do not need to be an internationally known evangelist to be a conduit of the Holy Spirit's transforming power. I have found people who often feel unqualified to pray for others because they are not on staff at the church, or because they have not been seminary-trained, or because they do not know the right words to pray. None of those things are necessary to pray for one another. As you gently lay your hand on a friend's shoulder and pray, the Holy Spirit has a point of contact to do his work of transformation in your friend's heart.

Confessing your sins to each other is a necessary part of praying for one another. Protestants typically recoil from the thought of hearing the confession of a fellow believer. For some Protestants, it sounds too Catholic. We rationalize our resistance to hear another's confession, because they do not need to go through another human being—whether a priest or lay person—in order to receive forgiveness. People can receive forgiveness of sin by taking their confession to God alone, but vocalizing sin to a Christian friend has powerful way of releasing sin's grip on the human heart. When you hear someone's confession, remember the following guidelines:

1) *Listen, don't lecture.* People who are coming to you with their confession typically know they are wrong. While they will require instruction regarding how to live differently, in the moment of their confession they need compassion not condemnation. Listening to them communicates your love, and it ultimately communicates God's love. Lecturing them will only compound their guilt. Listen carefully, intently, and empathetically.

2) *Don't look or sound shocked.* At times, people may come to you regarding a confession of a particular sin that is embarrassing. They may feel a great deal of shame regarding their sin, and a look of shock can send lightning bolts of judgment through their hearts. Do not be surprised at the depths of depravity. Human beings can be creative with their sin. Be prepared to hear their confession with a staid expression on your face.

3) *Suspend judgment.* It is easy to instantly judge people who are confessing their sin. Our minds quickly assume, "How could they do such a thing?" As they begin to unravel their confession, do not allow your mind or heart judge them. When the Pharisees flung the adulterous woman at the feet of Jesus, they wanted judgment. Jesus wrote in the dirt. He stood and replied not with judgment for the woman, but an indictment for the crowd. "If any one of you is without sin," Jesus said, "let him be the first to throw a stone at her" (John 8:7). He didn't ignore the woman's sin. Jesus just chose mercy over condemnation.

4) *Remind them that forgiveness is available.* Give them some degree of comfort by first reminding them that they are not alone. The reach of sin has not been shortened by education, money, or status, because all have sinned and fallen short of God's glory. The good news is that forgiveness of sin is available through the death, burial, and resurrection of Jesus. Remind them of promises like 1 John 1:9, "If we confess our sins, he is faithful and just and will forgive us our sins and purify us from all unrighteousness." Become a conduit of healing and real heart change by being a messenger of forgiveness.

5) *Pray for them.* Once you have listened to a friend's confession and extended the grace and forgiveness of God, then lift a heart-filled prayer. Do not worry about saying the right words. Simply ask God to forgive your friend. Ask the Holy Spirit to continue changing your friend's heart.

TEACH ONE ANOTHER

The Spirit creates shape shifters in the context of Christian community through the art of teaching. God gives some people the spiritual gift of teaching. I have been a steward of this spiritual gift, and I work hard to use my teaching gift to bring real life change in people's lives. While I believe in the spiritual gift of teaching, the Bible calls us all to teach one another. Gifted teachers have a responsibility to use their gift of teaching, but every Christian has the opportunity to teach others.

In order to fulfill the command to teach one another, you need the word of Christ to dwell in you richly.[9] I recommend the following regimen in order to allow the words of Scripture to live large in your heart.

1) *Listen to Spirit-empowered, Bible teaching on a regular basis.* Christians living in North America have a tremendous wealth of Christian resources. We are surrounded by good teaching which is readily available on Christian radio, CDs produced by local churches, and sermons available online by podcast or other web-based media. Do not pay much attention to teaching that is not Christianized self-help. Listen to teaching that is saturated with Scripture.

2) *Read good Christian books.* If you do not like to read, then ask the Holy Spirit to change your heart and mind and give you a desire to read. The digital age has made it simple to search, find, and order good Christian books. Ask your pastor to recommend good books by reputable Christian authors.

3) *Attend regular worship services where the Bible is taught.* When choosing a local church to attend, determine whether the Bible is taught in a compelling, passionate, and Spirit-empowered way. When you attend worship services, take your copy of the Bible, a notebook, and a pen. Take notes during the sermon. Following along in your own Bible and underline verses as you go along.

Allow the Scripture to live large in your heart, so you can be used by the Holy Spirit to teach others. You may not be given an opportunity to teach from the pulpit on Sunday morning, but the Bible says nothing about needing a microphone or a pulpit to teach. Let God's words live deep in your heart. Live out the heart of God's word in your life, and begin to teach it to others. This "one another" command is especially powerful when older men begin to teach young men, and older women begin to teach young women.[10]

SPUR ONE ANOTHER ON TOWARD LOVE AND GOOD DEEDS

The Christian life is an arduous, upward climb. God fills our lives with moments of victory and celebration. Every Sunday morning is a renewed celebration of the resurrection of Jesus. I am thankful for those moments of consolation. Nevertheless, moments of ease do not replace the ongoing toil of the Christian life. In this process of shape-shifting, we need constant encouragement.

Healthy local churches are places where we encourage one another and push one another along on the Jesus way. Sometimes encouragement is a pat on the back. We should be in competition with others to show appreciation to each other, especially for those who are working hard as volunteers in the local church. While encouragement is very often a pat on the back, sometimes encouragement is a kick in the pants.

My track coach in high school was Barry Reynolds, one of our English teachers and a professing Christian. He spurred me on to a lot of good deeds while I was in high school both on the track and in the classroom. After my conversion to Christ during my sophomore year, I become quite outspoken in my faith. I was in an English class during my junior year and a teacher asked us to read *Of Mice and Men* by John Steinbeck. I flipped through the book and noticed a number of times in which characters in the book took the Lord's name in vain. I explained to my teacher that I would not be able to read the book on moral grounds. She did not know how to respond to my zealous refusal to read the book. She talked to Coach Reynolds, and the next day he showed up to my class. He pulled me out in the hall and gave me a tongue lashing I will never forget. I explained to him my decision, and he called my bluff. He told me that I was using my faith to get out of school work, and such behavior was unbecoming for a Christian.

I was embarrassed because he was right. He rocked my world as he asked me to consider reading the book and writing a paper *from a*

Christian perspective. I finished the book that week and wrote my essay as a Christian critique of the book. I received a passing grade on the paper, but Coach Reynolds's words were more than mere encouragement. They shaped the direction of my life and ministry. I went on to become an English major in college and now reading, teaching, and writing have become my calling. His words of encouragement were not so much of appreciation as admonishment. The Holy Spirit used it to create a paradigm shift in me and change the direction my life.

LOVE ONE ANOTHER

No other "one another" command is more prevalent in the New Testament than the command to love one another. Jesus said, "A new command I give you: Love one another. As I have loved you, so you must love one another" (John 13:34). The greatest commands are to love God and love people. The "love one another" command is the standard by which all other "one another" commands are measured.

Love is the mark of the authentic community of Christians. Jesus said all men will know we are his disciples not because we have a fish on the bumper of our cars, not because we wear Christians T-shirts, not because we boycott homosexuals, not because we vote for elephants (or donkeys). Jesus said, "By this all men will know that you are my disciples, if you love one another" (John 13:35). In a community of love and self-sacrifice, the Spirit has freedom to work. When a local church loses focus on love for God and love for neighbor, the Holy Spirit becomes grieved and his work of transformation is hindered.

STUDY QUESTIONS

1. When you think about the doctrine of the Trinity are you drawn to the one God or the three persons—Father, Son, and Holy Spirit? Why?

2. How do you respond to people who claim to be Christians, but have no interest in the local church? What are the common excuses you hear from people who want to be Christians, but do not want to be a part of the local church?

3. What do you love most about your local church?

4. Who do you feel like you can be open with and ultimately submit to in your church?

5. What terrifies you the most about praying for other people?

6. What is the number one thing you can do to make the Scripture a greater part of your life, so you can begin to teach others?

7. What's the most meaningful encouragement you've received? Was is a pat on the back or a kick in the pants?

Chapter Eleven

SPIRITUAL PATHWAYS

*Listen, my son, and with your heart hear the principles of
your Master. Readily accept and faithfully follow the advice
of a loving Father, so that through the labor of obedience
you may return to Him from whom you have withdrawn
because of the laziness of disobedience.*

— BENEDICT OF NURSIA —

We who desire spiritual transformation can easily succumb to the
temptation to become lazy in the process. The Holy Spirit transforms us; we do not transform ourselves. Those of us who are becoming shape shifters are passive participants. We are both *passive* and *participants* in the Spirit's work. We do not change ourselves through legalism or self-righteous religion. Paul described legalists as "dogs" and self-righteousness as "dung".[1] Nevertheless, we can chose to partner with the Spirit and foster his work, or we can chose to hinder his work. The primary way we cooperate with the Spirit is by walking along spiritual pathways[2]. For centuries, Christians have walked down certain paths on the shapeshifting journey. As we walk along these ancient pathways, we join those who have experienced the transformation we seek.

Spiritual pathways are the classic spiritual disciplines, the well-trodden pathways walked by Christians from the historic and modern church. Walking down certain pathways does not change us. These spiritual disciplines put us in the place where the Spirit can transform us.[3] If we depend on our ability to walk along the spiritual pathways, we lose our dependence on the Holy Spirit. If we chose not to walk down any spiritual pathways, we become an obstacle to the Spirit. We walk down spiritual pathways whenever we practice any spiritual discipline that puts us in a place where we can receive from the Holy Spirit what we could not receive by direct effort.[4]

An innumerable number of spiritual pathways stand before us. The Psalmist writes, "Teach me your ways, O LORD, teach me your paths…" (Psalm 25:4). We learn not to walk one path, but many paths. Many of these pathways are considered classic, because they have been walked by so many before us. The following list of spiritual pathways has grown out of my own spiritual exploration. I have mastered none of them and I am particularly drawn to a few of them. I dislike some of these pathways, but walk along them all as I receive ongoing encouragement from the saints of the historic Church. The following are ten spiritual pathways I walk by the grace of God, and by walking along them, I increase my partnership with the Holy Spirit.

STILLNESS: *SLOWING IT DOWN*

The pace of life has sped up remarkably in the last sixty years. Consider the rapid growth of communication during this time. In 1948, the average American home had a telephone and radio. A few homes had a television. Today, the average middle class American home has high-speed internet access, a telephone line, a cell phone, radios, CD players, mp3 players, gaming systems, and televisions with satellite access. And these technological advances are just in a teenager's bedroom! We now have the ability to do more, work more, and accomplish more, but *doing* more does not mean we are *becoming* better people.

On seven occasions the Bible uses the phrase "be still."[5] A psalmist penned the most recognizable *be still* command. "Be still, and know that I am God; I will be exalted among the nations, I will be exalted in the earth" (Psalm 46:10). We do not quickly obtain the knowledge of God. The knowledge of God comes by "a long obedience in the same direction."[6] The Holy Spirit provides no short cut in the journey to transformation. Real transformation is a tediously slow process. If we continue to live life at breakneck speeds, we hinder the Spirit's work. The pathway of stillness requires that we steady our pace and slow down.

A few years ago, I determined to make a concerted effort to slow down. I knew that I was becoming too busy, and my own busyness had become a detriment to the Spirit's work of transformation in my inner life. I made the decision to drop the word "busy" from my vocabulary.

I needed to remove the word from my everyday speech, because I caught myself saying, "I am busy" simply to sound important. I had deceived myself into equating busyness with significance. Today, I struggle to remain on this pathway. As soon as I feel the pressures of life, work, and ministry prompting me to hurry up, I walk again along this pathway. I have made it a priority. We will not have time to walk down any other pathway, if we do not first walk down the pathway of stillness. We cannot find time; we must make time to be still.

SIMPLICITY: *CUTTING IT OUT*

Running parallel to the slow-paced stillness pathway is a much more narrowed pathway with fewer turns and fewer hills, a pathway called simplicity. In addition to slowing down the speed at which we live, we also need to cut certain things out. Paul writes to the church of Corinth with one of many warnings: "But I am afraid that just as Eve was deceived by the serpent's cunning, your minds may somehow be led astray from your sincere and pure devotion to Christ" (2 Corinthians 11:3). The phrase "sincere and pure devotion to Christ" is a poor translation. The New King James Version translates the phrase much more accurately. The NKJV uses the phrase "the simplicity that is in Christ."[7] When we walk down a pathway of simplicity, we cut out preoccupations and activities from our lives. We scale back. We begin to remove the things pulling us away from our highest priorities in life. We walk this pathway by simplifying in at least three areas—possessions, scheduling, and commitments.

(1) *Simplifying our possessions.* Jesus did not uphold the value of complete and utter detachment of things material or earthy, but he made it clear, "Life doesn't consist in the abundance of possessions" (Luke 12:15). The life we are carving out cannot be measured by the number of toys, even though popular opinion in American culture seems to go the opposite direction. Materialism can be best communicated in a bumper sticker I saw years ago. It read: "The one who ends up with most toys wins." To reframe it properly, the bumper sticker should read: "The one who ends up with the most toys *sins.*"

Having more material things does not equal more happiness in life. If you read the biography of any person of position or wealth, you can quickly see that while money can buy quite a number of pleasures, material comforts never bring lasting satisfaction. Honestly, the more *stuff* you have, the more *stress* you have, particularly in the digital age. I am a fan of electronic gadgets. I love laptop computers, cell phones, digital music players with built in Wi-Fi. The digital revolution has allowed us to communicate and share information in unbelievable ways. It is wonderful— that is, until something breaks. All of the electronic toys are great until batteries die, screens crack, or liquid spills on them. The more we have in our possession, the more we have to maintain. Think through your possessions and future purposes and ask if you need all these things. Then be strong, be bold and give some of it away.

(2) *Simplifying our schedule.* To my surprise, people living in small towns fill up their lives with just as much activity as people living in large metro areas. I have spent the last nine years living and pastoring in a small, rural Southern town. I hear people who come to visit talk about how refreshing the slower pace of life is here. I guess it all depends where you look. For me and my family, we constantly fight the temptation to overextend our weekly schedule.

I see packed schedules most often among parents who feel pressured to load up their kids' free time with activities out of fear that their beloved children may get into trouble. I have seen families sign their child up for every club, every social group, and every sport, and they end up living in their minivan. Our oldest son is a social animal. He loves being with people. He continually asks to join another group or sign up for another activity, and we have made our priorities clear. God comes first, followed by our family. After these two priorities, we participate in the life of our local church and do school work. Finally, we allow him to choose one sport per season. These priorities—God, family, church life, school work, and sports—do not leave much more time for anything else.

(3) *Simplify your commitments.* A person can only volunteer in so many places. Following Jesus requires choosing opportunities to serve others, but we can make only so many commitments. Relationships are highly valued components of our lives, but if we honestly reflect on them, we must admit that we can only keep up with so many relationships. If we do not create a few boundaries in our lives, we can over commit ourselves, or worse yet, we can double book ourselves, and then we begin to leave people in a difficult position.

In the first few years of my ministry, I doubled booked myself more than once. I fell into a trap of making commitments without consulting my calendar. I desired to serve and help when people asked, but by making two commitments for the same day and time, I would end up breaking one of those commitments. I have learned to never make a quick commitment. These days I always respond to a request with a quick, "Let me check my calendar and check with the boss (my wife) and get back to you." Walking down the pathway of simplicity requires simplifying your commitments. Before you say "yes" to one more thing, learn to flex your "no muscle." Learn to politely refuse the commitments requiring more time and energy than you have. Too many possessions, an over-loaded schedule, and over-extended commitments clutter up your soul and block the shape shifting work of the Spirit.

SILENCE & SOLITUDE: *TURNING IT OFF*

Silence and solitude together form one single pathway. You cannot have one without the other. You cannot experience silence without solitude, and solitude never becomes real without silence. When practiced together, these two spiritual disciplines construct a strong pathway where the Spirit can do his work of changing us.

This pathway is also one of the most difficult for me. I am rather introverted, but I am admittedly a participant in a media-saturated culture. I find silence and solitude a laborious path to walk.

Jesus walked the pathway of silence and solitude. Mark records a snapshot of a typical day for Jesus. "Very early in the morning, while it was still dark, Jesus got up, left the house and went off to a solitary place, where he prayed" (Mark 1:35). Most Christians rush right to the mention of prayer in this verse missing the crucial reference to a *solitary place*. Prayer is vital, but it is an altogether different pathway. Silence and solitude are something very distinct. We should frequent the prayer pathway. Nevertheless, times of prayer cannot replace times of silence and solitude.

I struggle with silence and solitude, because I am happily surrounded by noise in my world. Noise fills the typical home in America. We have TVs filling every room in the house with noise. We have digital music players filled with music and podcasts. Our vehicles come standard with radios and CD players. Our cell phones constantly ring or vibrate, both equally noisy, notifying us of calls, voice messages, and/or text messages. Most of us have computers or laptops which ding every time we have a new message in our inbox. Noise muddles our life with thoughts, images, and distractions. We need to walk a less cluttered path.

When you practice silence and solitude, the first discovery you will make is that you have a soul.[8] We can easily suppress our immaterial selves with noise. When we quiet our surroundings, our words, and our thoughts, we begin to realize the inner corridors of our hearts. I have to fight boredom and distraction, when I attempt to walk down a silent path. Solitude is easier to find. Silence requires me to refocus my attention on the Father, Son, and Holy Spirit. I have found it helpful to write down nagging thoughts, or things I need to do, or issues that rise to the surface on the silent road. Jotting down a few notes allows me to put them to the side so I can continue my walk. Once we settle into the silence, we are on a road of transformation.

FASTING: *LAYING IT DOWN*

In the spring of 2008, I led our church through Lent, the forty-day season of prayer and fasting before Resurrection Sunday. In instructing people on the ancient practice of Lent, I encouraged each person to determine how and when to fast, but to practice regular fasting for forty days in preparation for experiencing the joy of the resurrection. The number one report I heard from people after the Lenten season was how beneficial it was for them to have a structured way to fast. I agreed. Forcing myself to fast regularly allowed me to experience the Holy Spirit in a fresh and new way. After my second day of fasting during Lent, I wrote the following in my journal, *"Fasting is no fun. Fasting stinks, but it is good..."* I found no pleasure in hunger pains or caffeine withdrawal headaches. This pathway is not pleasurable, but it is good.

Fasting is not a commandment or a requirement. It is not a diet plan, although a person can lose weight from walking down the fasting pathway with some regularity. Fasting is not a way to show other people how spiritual you are; Jesus said to fast in secret.[9] Fasting is not a way to prove to God how spiritual you are. Fasting is not a hunger strike or a way to force God's hand to do what you want him to do. Conversely, fasting is a spiritual pathway, a road leading to a time of spiritual refocus. The Holy Spirit is able to transform us as we walk this road, because fasting is a way to expose our sin and fallenness. Richard Foster adds,

> *More than any other discipline, fasting reveals the things that control us. This is a wonderful benefit to the true disciple who longs to be transformed into the image of Jesus Christ. We cover up what is inside*

us with food and other good things, but in fasting these things surface.
If pride controls us, it will be revealed almost immediately.[10]

Fasting allows us to partner with the Spirit, because we tell our bodies that we will not be controlled by our appetites and our desires.

Prayer: *Turning it up*

People walk down the prayer pathway perhaps more than any other. Quite a number of skillful writers have published a number of wonderful books devoted to prayer.[11] I cannot claim any original insights on the prayer pathway, but I have discovered two common mistakes people make in their prayer lives.

(1) *Only asking God for material things.* People stumble on the prayer pathway by making prayer a time to rattle off their list of needs, and more tragically, their list of wants. When prayer becomes a matter of personal requests, the pathway takes a detour and leads the individual toward the kingdom of self and away from the kingdom of God. Certainly, it is appropriate to ask God for daily bread. He knows our needs, but he still wants us to ask him for daily provision. "You do not have, because you do not ask God" (James 4:2). We do not deviate from the path by asking for things in prayer. The problem begins when we only come to God in prayer to ask him for things. Jesus taught us to begin prayer with praise (*Our Father in heaven, hallowed by your name*) and a humble commitment to God's plan (*your kingdom come, your will be done*). When I am in a small group and we are going to have a time of prayer, I do not take prayer requests for this reason. Prayer requests in any kind of small group reinforce this common mistake.

(2) *Talking too much during prayer.* Prayer is a dialogue not a monologue. Our prayers should be two-way communication between us and God. I have found some people to be terrified by prayer, because they claim not to know what to say. I always encourage them not to worry. The Holy Spirit will help us pray. If I do not sense the leading of the Holy Spirit and I still have trouble voicing the right words, I have found praying the Psalms to be an effective way to communicate with the Triune God.

In addition to the help we receive from the Spirit and Scripture, prayer includes listening to voice of God. Jesus said, "My sheep listen to my voice; I know them, and they follow me" (John 10:27). We hear his voice through the words of Scripture, and the Holy Spirit speaks in a soft, still voice. Some of the most transformative moments of prayer occur when the Spirit speaks by conviction. He will indicate areas of our life that have become inconsistent with the Jesus way. He will talk to us about our future and encourage us in this journey of transformation.

READING: *EAT IT UP*

We do not read the Bible like we read any other book. We do not read it like a novel for entertainment. This kind of reading would lead us to *hedonism*, reading for pleasure. We do not read it like a textbook in order to pass a test. This kind of reading would lead us to *intellectualism*, reading to increase only in knowledge. We do not read it like an owner's manual to learn how to do something. This kind of reading would lead us to *pragmatism*, living by what works rather than what is right. We do not read it like a catalogue to pick out what you want. This kind of reading would lead us to *consumerism*, a reading to meet a need. We read it to live.

Ancient Christians used the Latin phrase *lectio divina* to describe this spiritual pathway. This kind of reading is *spiritual reading*. It is more akin to eating than reading. We hold the holy book in our hands, and we eat it.[12] The weeping Jewish prophet Jeremiah used a similar metaphor: "When your words came, I ate them; they were my joy and my heart's delight, for I bear your name, O LORD God Almighty" (Jeremiah 15:16). We walk down this pathway of spiritual reading as we consume the Scripture.

Read it slowly, frequently, and prayerfully. Chew on it. Enjoy it like a juicy steak. Do not gobble it down like a plate of chicken wings. Do not over-indulge on the sweetness of the sacred text. Some Christians pride themselves on reading the Bible in one year, but for most people such a Bible reading plan is far too rushed. Do not try to read four chapters a day. Instead focus your time chewing on four verses a day.

Think about what you are reading. Allow it to roll around in the corners of your imagination. Talk to God about what you are eating. Allow this reading pathway to intersect with the prayer pathway. Digest it. Eating the book puts us on a pathway where the Holy Spirit can change us through Holy Scripture. Let the Scripture become a part of your life.

REFLECTING: *THINKING IT OVER*

As I completed my doctor of ministry dissertation, I was fortunate to have the opportunity to sit down with twenty pastors and ask them questions about how they experienced the Holy Spirit work of transformation.[13] When I asked them about the spiritual pathways (spiritual disciplines) they walked, I received twenty-five different responses. Any spiritual activity can become a spiritual pathway, so the list could be unending. Nearly all of the pastors described prayer and Bible reading, but only four of the twenty mentioned reflection or meditation.

According to Thomas Merton, reflection has two distinct functions—one outward and one inward. The outward function of reflection is to reflect upon the nature and personhood of God, to become aware of the presence of God.[14] This kind of reflection includes thinking God's thoughts after him through the practice of spiritual reading. The inward expression of reflection is one of the most overlooked pathways in the modern church. The inward function of reflection is the practice of reflecting upon one's own inner life. It is the process of prayerfully thinking through one's motivations, attitude, emotional condition and thoughts. When people become aware of the vast caverns of their inner life, then they begin to discover their real self, the self that God created them to be, a self that reflects the image of Christ. *How are we ever to know what the Spirit is doing to change our hearts if we never take a peek inside?* Inward reflection is not intended to awaken a person to a self-absorbed egoism, but it entails, as Merton remarks, "awakening our interior self and attuning ourselves inwardly to the Holy Spirit, so that we will be able to respond to His grace."[15] Walking the pathway of reflection, particularly inward reflection, puts us in a powerful place to be changed by the Spirit.

WRITING: *JOTTING IT DOWN*

Over the years I have tried and failed to keep a journal. I have tried to record my thoughts in cheap spiral notebooks and fancy looking leather journals, but all my attempts led to failure. My problem has been that I have tried to keep a daily diary. I have tried to record thoughts every day, and if I miss a day, a week, or a month, then I get frustrated and throw the notebook in the trash. Recently, I have purchased a certain kind of journal, and I thought I would try again. On this most recent journey down the writing and journaling pathway, I have set no rules, no guidelines, and no daily requirements. I may write in it every day for a week, and then I may not write anything in it for weeks. I record quotes I have read, prayers I am unable to vocalize, and thoughts as I have walked on the reflection pathway.

The writing pathway has been blazed in unison with other pathways. For me, reflection and writing go together. I have experienced great benefit in reflecting, both outwardly and inwardly, and journaling my thoughts. At times, I jot down just a few thoughts. Other times I write for pages and pages. Those moments feel as if my own thinking is infused by the Spirit. When I write in times of inward reflection, the writing turns into moments of worship and sincere confession and repentance. At this junction, writing intersects with prayer. Many times I have written down my prayers with all the passion of verbal prayer. Writing leaves a written record for us to track our growth, and it is a useful tool in the hands of the Spirit.

SINGING: *LETTING IT OUT*

Singing is a spiritual pathway whether you have the ability to sing or not. You may not be invited to join the worship team or choir at your church, but singing your praise to God puts you in a place where God the Holy Spirit can change you on the inside. Not just any kind of singing puts you on this pathway. Singing in the shower may be a great way to start the day, but this pathway refers to congregational singing in a corporate worship service. In our worship services, we keep the amps cranked up. We are perhaps not the loudest church in worship on Sunday morning, but we do keep the volume at a relatively high level so people feel comfortable singing out loud.

Dietrich Bonhoeffer, the German pastor who was executed by the Nazis in 1945, continued to hold worship services in his concentration camp before his death. On one occasion he was asked, "Why do Christians sing when they are together?" His response was profound.

The reason is, quite simply, because in singing together it is possible for them to speak and pray the same Word at the same time; in other words, because here they can unite in the Word.[16]

Singing with other Christians in congregational worship creates a certain kind of unity whereby the Spirit is free to blow through our lives like a mighty rushing wind.

Nothing grieves me more than seeing people sitting down and not participating during our time of singing in our Sunday morning worship service. In our tradition, we typically sing six or seven contemporary worship songs, and we stand during the entire time. I understand some people have physical needs preventing them from standing. But most people who are sitting down do not lack the strength. They lack the knowledge concerning how powerful the spiritual pathway of singing can be.

Singing praise to God humbles us. Some of my shape-shifting encounters with the Holy Spirit have occurred while I was singing. When I was a freshman in college, I grew my hair out long. I am embarrassed to admit that I had to blow dry it and feather it back on the sides to keep it out of my face. On one occasion, I attended a worship service with some friends. While we were singing, I sensed the Holy Spirit nudging me to get on my knees and sing with my face on the ground. My first thought was, "What about my hair?" Absurd, I know, but this reaction was my first thought. After wrestling with his inner prompting, I knelt down and sang with my face in the carpet. The Holy Spirit humbled me in a powerful experience of transformation while I was on the singing pathway.

CONFESSION & REPENTANCE: *DOING IT OVER*

No other pathway has led to more moments of transformation than the pathway of confession and repentance. They complement each other and must be practiced together. Confession without repentance is mere talk. Repentance without confession is mere superficial change. When practiced in harmony, confession and repentance form a crucial pathway leading us to spiritual transformation. Other pathways may be optional; this pathway is not. If we chose not to walk this pathway on a regular basis, we cannot expect the Spirit to transform us into the image of Jesus for the Father's joy. No matter how painful and heart-wrenching this pathway may be, it is essential.

Confession is "saying the same thing." John writes, "If we confess our sins, he is faithful and just and will forgive us our sins and purify us from all unrighteousness" (1 John 1:9). The Greek word translated "confess" comes from two Greek words—*homo* meaning "same" and *logos* meaning "words." To confess our sin is to say the same thing God says about it. He is calls it sin, and by our confession we agree with him that it is sin. If we desire the Spirit's power to transform us, then we must be honest with our own sin and fallenness. We need to stop rationalizing our sin. We need to expose it to the light of God's truth and call it what it is: sin.

Repentance means "doing things differently the next time." The Greek word translated "repent" is *metanoeo* meaning "rethink." When we confess our sin, we verbally acknowledge it as such. Repentance means to rethink your life in light of God's truth. On the pathway of confession and repentance, rethinking leads to reliving. The expectation of rethinking and developing a plan to do things differently is to lead invariably to a different kind of lifestyle.

Mastering these pathways requires understanding them in more depth than I can cover in this chapter.[17] We walk these pathways as we practice the classic spiritual disciplines. The term "discipline" does not imply pleasure. I encourage you to delay gratification while walking on these pathways. They require discipline, much like an Olympic athlete. Do not *try* to walk these pathways—rather, train yourself to walk them. What we cannot accomplish by trying, we can by training.[18] Let's agree together to quit *trying* to be shape shifters. Let's agree to quit *trying* to become like Christ. Instead let's commit to train ourselves to walk these spiritual pathways, and allow the Holy Spirit to transform us into the perfect image of Jesus for the joy of God the Father through the local church.

STUDY GUIDE

1. What is the difference between trying and training?

2. What do you need to do to slow down the pace of your life?

3. What do you need to cut out of your life in order to simplify? Is it possessions, activities, relationships, commitments or something else?

4. What is one creative way to carve out time for silence and solitude?

5. What is your experience with fasting? What would it take to cause you to fast with more regularity?

6. What kind of prayer and Bible reading routine works best for you?

7. When was the last time you spent time reflecting on your own heart, your attitude, and motivations? What do you need to do in order to spend more time in reflection?

8. Which is harder for you, writing or singing? Which do you need to give more attention to in your life?

9. What one thing in your life do you need to confess as sin and develop a plan to repent?

NOTES

INTRODUCTION

1   G.K. Chesterton, *Orthodoxy*, Reprint (New York: Doubleday, 2001), 46.

CHAPTER ONE

1   Mark 6:12

2   Acts 2:38

3   Revelation 2:2-3

4   Dietrich Bonhoeffer, *The Cost of Discipleship*, (New York: Touchstone, 1995), 89.

5   See Ken Collins, *Exploring Christian Spirituality*, (Grand Rapids: Baker, 2000). Collins has compiled a good overview of Christian spirituality from a variety of theological traditions. Collins regrettably did not include a section on Pentecostal/ charismatic spirituality, which I believe is an important and influential spiritual- ity in the church today. See Steven Land, *Pentecostal Spirituality: A Passion for the Kingdom*, (London: Sheffield Academic, 1993), for a deeper understanding of Pentecostal/charismatic spirituality.

6   Gordon Fee, *Listening to the Spirit*, (Grand Rapids: Eerdmans, 2000), 5.

7   Paul does use the word "repentance" or "repented" in Romans 2:4, 2 Corinthians 7:9, 7:10, 12:21 and 2 Timothy 2:25.

8   Technically the geometrid caterpillar becomes a vividly-colored moth which to the untrained eye looks like a butterfly.

9   For a fuller description of the term "transformation" see Dallas Willard, *Renova- tion of the Heart*, (Colorado Springs: NavPress, 2002), 14.

10 Willard discusses these three descriptions in "Spiritual Formation in Christ: A Perspective on What It Is and How It Might Be Done." *Journal of Psychology and Theology* 28.4 (2000): 254-258.

11 http://www2.oprah.com/index.jhtml

12 Roger Olson discusses the "dark side" of the Pentecostal/charismatic movement including sexual and financial scandals within Pentecostalism in *The Christian Century*, March 7, 2006, 27-30.

13 While Pentecostals and charismatics have been rather silent on the subject of spiritual transformation, Simon Chan has offered helpful direction in the area of spiritual theology. He writes from a Pentecostal/charismatic perspective with an ecumenical vision. See Simon Chan, *Spiritual Theology: A Systematic Study of the Christian Life*, (Downers Grove, IL: InterVarsity, 1998).

14 Nicene Creed 381 AD

CHAPTER TWO

1 John 16:13

2 Ephesians 5:18-19

3 Luther, Martin, "Preface to the Epistle of St. Paul to the Romans," *Martin Luther, Selections from His Writings*, Ed. John Dillenberger, (New York: Anchor Books, 1962), 19.

4 1 Corinthians 3:16

CHAPTER THREE

1 Larry Hart, *Truth Aflame*, (Nashville: Thomas Nelson, 1999), 2. Dr. Larry Hart was the systematic theology professor who announced in class that we were all theologians. See also Stanley Grenz & Roger Olsson, *Who Needs Theology?: An Invitation to the Study of God*, (Downers Grove, IL: InterVarsity, 1996).

2 See Robert Louis Wilken, *The Spirit of Early Christian Thought*, (New Haven: Yale University Press, 2003), 106.

3 Augustine, *On the Trinity*, 15:28:1

4 See Hart, *Truth Aflame*, 66ff.

5 *Brown-Driver-Briggs' Hebrew Definitions* (adar)

6 J.B. Phillips, *Your God is Too Small*, (New York: Macmillian, 1961), 8.

7 1 Corinthians 13:1

8 The concept that the God of the Old Testament is not the God of the New Testament is still around in popular forms. It is also a reference to second-century Marcionism, an early church heresy teaching the same concept. Marcion was an early Christian teacher who was excommunicated for teaching that the Christian faith was in opposition to the Jewish faith. He rejected the authority of Old Testament Scriptures and taught that the God of the Old Testament was a lesser God than the Father of Jesus.

9 Donald McCullough, *The Trivialization of God*, (Colorado Springs: NavPress, 1995), 14.

CHAPTER FOUR

1 The name used in Isaiah 14:12 in Hebrew is *haylale*, which is translated "morning star." *Lucifer* is not an English translation of the devil's name, but it is the Latin translation of the Hebrew word for "morning star." In Latin, it is the masculine, singular form of *lucidus* meaning "shining, bright, clear." Unfortunately, the translators of the King James Version brought the Latin word into the English text and capitalized it, giving people the impression that the Latin word *lucifer* is a name for the devil.

2 Early church leaders such as Origen, Jerome, and Augustine all attributed this reference to the devil. Augustine wrote, "The words of Isaiah, 'How Lucifer, son of the dawn, has fallen from the sky' [Isa. 14:12] and the rest, which are spoken about, or to, one and the same person under the guise of the King of Babylon, are certainly in the actual context understood of the devil." Augustine *On Christian Teaching*, Trans. by R.P.H. Green, (New York: Oxford University Press, 1997), 99.

3 Luke 10:18

4 I learned the map and compass in the 1980s before the miracle of portable GPS devices. GPS makes the whole orientation process a lot easier.

5 Luke 17:21

6 Two teams have formed on how to interpret Romans 7. The first team interprets this passage as Paul's reflection on his life before Christ. The second team interprets the passage as Paul's post-conversion, present struggle with sin. Irenaeus, Tertullian, Origen, Ambrose, John Chrysostom, John Wesley, G. Campbell Morgan, A. T. Robertson, F. L. Godet, James Denney, Anthony Hoekema, Paul Achtemeier, Gordon Fee, N. T. Wright, Joseph Fitzmyer, and Douglas Moo argue the Roman 7 passage refers to Paul's life before Christ. Augustine, Martin Luther, John Calvin, Matthew Henry, C. I. Scofield, D. Martyn Lloyd-Jones, John Murray, John Walvoord, F. F. Bruce, C. E. B. Cranfield, John R. W. Stott, Kent Hughes, Warren Wiersbe, Charles Swindoll, Charles Ryrie, David Needham, J. I. Packer, and James D. G. Dunn each argue that Roman 7 refers to Paul's present life with Christ.

7 G.K. Chesterton, *Orthodoxy*, Reprint, (New York: Doubleday, 2001), 75.

8 Eugene Peterson, *Eat This Book: A Conversation in the Art of Spiritual Reading*, (Grand Rapids: Eerdmans, 2006), 31.

CHAPTER FIVE

1 "The Soup Nazi" is episode 115 of *Seinfeld* written by Spike Feresten. http://www.seinfeldscripts.com/TheSoupNazi.htm

2 Modalism is also called Sabellianism, after Sabellius, the third century theologian who taught that God is one nature and one person. His theological position was refuted by Tertullian who introduced the word "trinity" to the Church. A form of modalism exists today among the oneness Pentecostals such as the United Pentecostal Church International which teaches that biblical titles "Father, Son and Holy Spirit" are not distinct persons but "offices, roles, or relationship to humanity."

3 Darrell Johnson, *Experiencing the Trinity*, (Vancouver: Regent College Publishing, 2002), 14.

4 See Matthew 3:16–17, 28:19; Mark 1:10–11; Luke 1:35, 3:22; John 1:32, 14:26; Acts 2:33; 2 Corinthians 13:14; Hebrews 9:14; 1 John 5:7–8.

5 As quoted by Philip Schaff, *History of the Christian Church* Vol. 2, (Peabody, MA: Hendrickson, 1996), 247.
6 Ibid, 249.
7 See the complete Nicene Creed from 381 AD in the appendix section.
8 Luke Timothy Johnson, *The Creed: What Christians Believe and Why it Matters*, (New York: Doubleday, 2003), 77.
9 G.K. Chesterton, *Orthodoxy*, Reprint (New York: Doubleday, 2001), 45.
10 Stephen Seamands and Michael Pasquarello at Asbury Theological Seminary were the first people who introduced me to the concept of Trinitarian grammar. See Steve Seamands, *Ministry in the Image of God*, 11 and Michael Pasquarello, *Christian Preaching: A Trinitarian Theology of Proclamation*, (Grand Rapids: Baker, 2007), 40.
11 James B. Torrance, *Worship, Community & The Triune God of Grace*, (Downers Grove, IL: InterVarsity, 1996), 22.

CHAPTER SIX

1 James B. Torrance, Worship, *Community & the Triune God of Grace*, (Downers Grove, IL: InterVarsity, 1997), 31.
2 Augustine's Trinitarian model of *lover, loved, and love* has formed a theological launching pad for others to build upon it. Karl Barth used similar categories to describe the Triune God as *revealer, revealed, and the revelation itself* (i.e. God himself reveals himself through himself).
3 Darrell Johnson, *Experiencing the Trinity*, (Vancouver: Regent College Publishing, 2002), 61.
4 "It's Alright Ma (I'm Only Bleeding)" Written by Bob Dylan, copyright ©1965; renewed 1993 Special Rider Music.
5 Stephen Seamands, *Ministry in the Image of God: The Trinitarian Shape of Christian Service*, (Downers Grove, IL: InterVarsity Press, 2005), 103.
6 Johnson, 54.
7 Ibid.
8 The terms "reformed," "evangelical," and "charismatic" are difficult to define and many Christians would describe themselves in terms of some combination of all three. I am using these terms in a very subjective way. "Reformed" describes those Christians with a high-view of sovereignty of God, particularly as related to salvation. "Evangelical" describes Christians who place a high value on evangelism and missions. "Charismatics" describes fellow believers who believe all of the gifts of the Holy Spirit are active in the church today.
9 Reformed Christians are certainly Christ-centered. For me the reformed tradition aligns itself with the Father, because it is from this tradition that I have developed a much stronger appreciation of the sovereignty and providence of God.
10 I first developed this Trinitarian model of spiritual transformation in my Doctor of Ministry dissertation. Derek E. Vreeland, "The Relationship between Spiritual

Transformation and Leadership Growth in a Pentecostal/Charismatic Context" (D.Min. diss., Asbury Theological Seminary, 2007), 24-26.

11 L.T. Jeyachandran, "The Trinity as a Paradigm for Spiritual Transformation," *Beyond Opinion: Living the Faith We Defend*, Ed. Ravi Zacharias, (Nashville: Thomas Nelson, 2007), 247.

12 Romans 8:29

CHAPTER SEVEN

1 Ephesians 1:9

2 Matthew 11:25-26

3 See John Piper, *The Pleasures of God*, (Sisters, OR: Multnomah, 1991), 25.

4 John 15:8

5 http://www.ccel.org/ccel/edwards/trinity/files/trinity.html

6 John 5:20; See also John 3:35; 10:17; 15:9; and 17:24

7 http://www.reformed.org/documents/WSC_frames.html

8 John Piper, *The Dangerous Duty of Delight*, (Sisters, OR: Multnomah, 2001), 20.

CHAPTER EIGHT

1 In the NIV, the title "Christ" appears in the New Testament 541 times. The name "Jesus" appears 1,275 times in the New Testament.

2 http://www.rottentomatoes.com/m/passion_of_the_christ/

3 Jon Meacham, "From Jesus to Christ," *Newsweek* March 28, 2005.

4 The Nicene Creed was originally adopted in 325 AD at the council of Nicaea. It was expanded at the Council of Constantinople in 381. This quotation is from the expanded form of the creed.

5 http://ldsfaq.byu.edu/view.asp?q=178

6 Anne Rice, *Christ the Lord: Road to Cana*, (New York: Knopf, 2008).

7 N.T. Wright, *Simply Christian*, (New York: HarperCollins, 2006), 91

8 Jean-Marie Hamel, *Living From the Inside Out*, (New York: Harmony, 2004), 23.

9 1 Corinthians 2:16

10 Dallas Willard, *Renovation of the Heart: Putting on the Character of Christ*, (Colorado Springs: NavPress, 2002), 87.

11 Philippians 2:5

12 Romans 5:5

13 "Welcoming back John Mark" is a reference to the disagreement between Paul and Barnabas (Acts 15:37-40).

CHAPTER NINE

1 Gordon Fee, *Paul, the Spirit, and the People of God*, (Peabody, MA: Hendrickson, 1996), 26.

2 Dallas Willard, *Renovation of the Heart: Putting on the Character of Christ*, (Colorado Springs: NavPress, 2002), 22.

3 While Dallas Willard describes spiritual transformation as a "Spirit-driven process" he has little to say concerning what the Holy Spirit is actually doing to conform us into the image of Jesus. There has been very little written on the Spirit's activity in spiritual transformation. My work in this chapter only scratches the surface on the work of the Spirit in the human heart.

4 C.S. Lewis, *The Weight of Glory and Other Addresses*, (New York: HarperOne, 2001), 26.

5 Philippians 2:13 (*The Amplified Bible*)

6 John 16:13

7 Freedom in Christ Ministries has put together a wonderful list of new names, new identities under the title, "Who I am In Christ." http://www.ficm.org/whoiam.htm

8 http://www.ccel.org/ccel/edwards/affections.iv.html

9 Peter Scazzero, *Emotionally Healthy Spirituality: Unleash a Revolution in Your Life in Christ*, (Nashville: Integrity, 2006), 72.

CHAPTER TEN

1 Nearly all Christian churches adhere to the doctrines contained in the Apostles' Creed and the Nicene Creed. The origins of the Apostles' Creed are unclear, but we have historical records which indicate people would memorize and recite the Apostles' Creed at their baptism. The Nicene Creed was formed in 325 AD. and then expanded at the Council of Constantinople in 381 AD. The Nicene Creed, although longer than the Apostle's Creed, contains a Trinitarian structure. See the appendix section for the 381 AD edition of the Nicene Creed.

2 See 1 Timothy 3:1-7 for the qualifications for church leaders

3 The term "universal Church" is not found in the New Testament. In the writings of Paul, we see images of a "heavenly church" which matches the description of the Universal Church. See Robert Banks, *Paul's Idea of Community*, (Peabody, MA: Hendrickson, 1994), 39.

4 The Nicene Creed describes the Church as "one holy catholic and apostolic." The word "catholic" does not mean Roman Catholic. Rather it means "universal." I am using the phrase "universal Church" instead of "Catholic Church," so as not to confuse the issue with Roman Catholicism.

5 I am indebted to Mark Driscoll for making this point time and time again concerning Jesus' position as the chief shepherd and senior pastor. Jesus is the senior pastor of the universal Church and therefore should also be the Senior Pastor of our local churches. http://theresurgence.com/mark_driscoll_2008-02-26_video_tnc_the_ox--qualifications_of_a_church_planter

6 John Calvin, *The Institutes of the Christian Religion*, IV.1.9.

7 See Richard C. Meyer, *One Anothering*, (San Diego: LuraMedia, 1990); Richard C. Meyer, *One Anothering, Volume 2*, (Philadelphia: Innisfree, 1999); Richard C. Meyer, *One Anothering, Volume 3*, (Philadelphia: Innisfree, 2002).

8 Biblical submission and accountability can be with an individual or with a group. A small group is best, because different people can provide different perspectives on your private struggle.

9 "Let the word of Christ dwell in you richly as you teach and admonish one another"... (Colossians 3:16)

10 See Titus 2

CHAPTER ELEVEN

1 Paul referred to the legalistic Judaizers, those Jews who required Gentiles to be circumcised in addition to faith in Christ, as dogs (Philippians 3:2). He also compared any kind of self-righteous religion to dung, because nothing could compare to the value of knowing Jesus by grace through faith (Philippians 3:8).

2 I am indebted to Gary Thomas for the "pathway" metaphor. See Gary Thomas, *Sacred Pathways*, (Grand Rapids: Zondervan, 2000).

3 See Richard Foster, *Celebration of Discipline*, (San Francisco: Harper, 1998), 8.

4 Dallas Willard does not use the metaphor of "pathways," but has developed the most compelling definition of "spiritual disciplines." He defines them as "an activity within our power—something we can do—that brings us to a point where we can do what we at present cannot do by direct effort." Dallas Willard, *The Great Omission*, (San Francisco: HarperOne, 2006), 150.

5 Be still and watch (Exodus 14:14); be still and rest (Nehemiah 8:11); be still and wait (Psalm 37:7); be still and know (Psalm 46:10); be still and back off (Jeremiah 46:6); be still and expect (Zechariah 2:10-13); and be still and believe (Mark 4:39).

6 Eugene Peterson redeemed this statement taken from Friedrich Nietzsche's, *Beyond Good and Evil*. Nietzsche writes, "The essential thing 'in heaven and earth' is...that there should be long obedience in the same direction; there thereby results, and has always resulted in the long run, something which has made life worth living." See Eugene Peterson, *Long Obedience in the Same Direction: Discipleship in an Instant Society*, 1980, (Downers Grove: IL: InterVarsity Press, 2000), 17.

7 The word "simplicity" in the NKJV is carried over from the KJV. The NLT uses
   the phrase "simple devotion." The NASB employs the word "simplicity" in its
   translation of the verse. The Greek word *aplotes*, translated "simplicity" in the
   NKJV and NASB was originally used to convey singleness. The English word
   "sincerity" tends to imply whole-heartedness of motivation , while "simplicity"
   implies a reduction of number.

8 Dallas Willard made a similar statement in a series of lectures delivered in 2001
   at Regent College in Vancouver, British Columbia. See Dallas Willard, *Leadership
   and Spirituality* (Audio CD), (Vancouver: Regent Audio, 2001).

9 Matthew 6:16-18

10 Richard Foster, *Celebration of Discipline*, (San Francisco: Harper, 1998), 69.

11 The most influential book on prayer in my journey of spiritual transformation
   has been Richard Foster, *Prayer: Finding the Heart's True Home*, (San Francisco:
   Harper, 1992). This book captures Foster's ecumenical vision by describing twen-
   ty-one different kinds of prayers drawn from contemplative, holiness, charismatic,
   social justice, evangelical, and incarnational streams of the Christian faith.

12 See Eugene Peterson, *Eat This Book: A Conversation in the Art of Spiritual Reading*, (Grand Rapids: Eerdmans, 2006).

13 See Derek E. Vreeland, "The Relationship between Spiritual Transformation and
   Leadership Growth in a Pentecostal/Charismatic Context" (D.Min. diss., Asbury
   Theological Seminary, 2007).

14 Thomas Merton, *Seeds* (Boston: Shambhala, 2002), 81.

15 Ibid, 79.

16 Dietrich Bonhoeffer, *Life Together: The Classic Exploration of Faith in Community*, (San Francisco: HarperOne, 1978), 59.

17 To understand spiritual pathways/spiritual disciplines with greater depth, I recommend Richard Foster, *Celebration of Discipline*, (San Francisco: Harper, 1998).

18 John Ortberg writes, "(Training) means to arrange your life around certain
   exercises and experiences that will enable you to do eventually what you are not
   yet able to do even by trying hard." John Ortberg, et. al., *Growth: Training vs.
   Trying*, (Grand Rapids: Zondervan, 2000), 4.

NICENE CREED 381 AD

We believe in one God,
the Father, the Almighty,
maker of heaven and earth,
of all that is, seen and unseen.

We believe in one Lord, Jesus Christ,
the only Son of God,
eternally begotten of the Father,
God from God, Light from Light,
true God from true God,
begotten, not made, of one Being with the Father.

Through him all things were made.
For us and for our salvation
he came down from heaven:
by the power of the Holy Spirit
he became incarnate from the Virgin Mary,
and was made man.
For our sake he was crucified under Pontius Pilate;
he suffered death and was buried.

On the third day he rose again
in accordance with the Scriptures;
he ascended into heaven
and is seated at the right hand of the Father.
He will come again in glory to judge the living and the dead,
and his kingdom will have no end.

We believe in the Holy Spirit, the Lord, the giver of life,
who proceeds from the Father and the Son.
With the Father and the Son he is worshiped and glorified.
He has spoken through the Prophets.

We believe in one holy catholic and apostolic Church.
We acknowledge one baptism for the forgiveness of sins.
We look for the resurrection of the dead,
and the life of the world to come.

Amen.

Appendix 2

RECOMMENDED READING
FOR FURTHER STUDY

Cantalamessa, Raniero. *Come, Creator Spirit: Meditations on the Veni Creator*. Collegeville, MN: Liturgical, 2003.

Chan, Simon. *Spiritual Theology: A Systematic Study of the Christian Life*. Downers Grove, IL: InterVarsity, 1998.

Collins, Kenneth J., ed. *Exploring Christian Spirituality: An Ecumencial Reader*. Grand Rapids: Baker, 2000.

Foster, Richard. *Celebration of Discipline: The Path to Spiritual Growth*. 1978. San Francisco: Harper, 1998.

Foster, Richard. *Prayer: Finding the Heart's True Home*. San Francisco: Harper, 1992.

Johnson, Darrell E. *Experiencing the Trinity*. Vancouver: Regent College, 2002.

Johnson, Luke Timothy. *The Creed: What Christians Believe and Why It Matters*. New York: Doubleday, 2003.

Kempis, Thomas á. *The Imitation of Christ*. Trans. Joseph N. Tylenda. New York: Vintage Books, 1998.

McNeal, Reggie. *A Work of Heart: Understanding How God Shapes Spiritual Leaders*. New York: Jossey-Bass, 2000.

Menzies, William W. and Robert P. Menzies. *Spirit and Power: Foundations of Pentecostal Experience*. Grand Rapids: Zondervan, 2000.

Merton, Thomas. *Seeds*. Ed. Robert Inchausti. Boston: Shambhala, 2002.

Mulholland, M. Robert, Jr. *The Deeper Journey: The Spirituality of Discovering Your True Self*. Downers Grove, IL: InterVarsity, 2006.

Peterson, Eugene. *Eat This Book: A Conversation in the Art of Spiritual Reading*. Grand Rapids: Eerdmans, 2006.

Scazzero, Peter L. *Emotionally Healthy Spirituality: Unleash a Revolution in Your Life in Christ*. Nashville: Integrity, 2006.

Schaeffer, Francis A. *True Spirituality: How to Live for Jesus Moment by Moment*. 1971. Carol Stream, IL: Tyndale, 2001.

Seamands, Stephen. *Ministry in the Image of God: The Trinitarian Shape of Christian Service*. Downers Grove, IL: InterVarsity, 2005.

Tan, Siang-Yang and Douglas H. Gregg. *Disciplines of the Holy Spirit: How to Connect to the Spirit's Power and Presence*. Grand Rapids: Zondervan 1997.

Thomas, Gary. *The Beautiful Fight*. Grand Rapids: Zondervan, 2007.

Torrance, James B. *Worship, Community and the Triune God of Grace*. Downers Grove, IL: InterVarsity, 1996.

Ware, Bruce A. *Father, Son, & Holy Spirit: Relationships, Roles, & Relevance*. Wheaton, IL: Crossway, 2005.

Willard, Dallas. *Renovation of the Heart: Putting on the Character of Christ*. Colorado Springs: NavPress, 2002.

Willard, Dallas. *The Great Omission: Reclaiming Jesus's Essential Teachings on Discipleship*. San Francisco: Harper, 2006.